The Revelation of God

A Bible Study Workbook

Book 1

'Covenant'

Derek Williams

All material in this work book is copyright © Derek Williams 2010.

This work book may not be copied in any fashion, distributed, loaned, published or sold in any manner whatsoever, not for any reason without the prior written permission of Derek Williams.

About the author

Derek Williams is a Catholic Evangelist whose primary calling is to teach the Word of God in the power of the Spirit. He has been doing this since 1990, but on a full-time basis since 2003. He is married to Lynn and they have four children.

For further information and other bible resources please contact Derek via:-
derekbdiv@gmail.com

Cover design by Steve O'Brien
Crucified christ: http://freechristimages.org entitled 'it is finished' Christ on the Cross
Diego Velazquez, 1632
Used with permission

Contents

Introduction

This Bible study workbook has been written for anybody who wants to read the bible but is having trouble understanding what it is all about. It can either be used as a guide in itself for individual study and/or group study; or with an accompanying set of cd's. The cd's were recorded in a Church environment.

Outline

The first two chapters treat of the marriage covenant and the nine steps to a Hebrew blood covenant ritual. The bible is all about 'covenant'. Once you gain the understanding of what a covenant is the bible will be a lot more accessible. Following this the workbook will take you through God's covenants with Adam, Noah, Abraham, Moses, David and finally the new and everlasting covenant in the blood of Jesus.

Throughout the course you will be invited to write in the book. Please write out the full scripture and answer the appropriate questions if you can. This is very important to help you remember and understand the scriptures. It is one thing to read a sentence, quite another to reproduce it. You will need to keep a bible to hand at all times. The questions and quotes are based on the New American Bible and the New Jerusalem Bible. Some translations may not quote exactly the same scripture references so you will need to be very aware of this if you are using a different translation. Also, some translations do not have books of the Bible that are in the Catholic version. For example the book of Wisdom is in the New American Bible but not in the New International Version.

Where the Catholic Catechism is quoted I have abbreviated it with CCC.

God's Word

Before you begin with this study please remember this is God's Word you are studying. Hence it should be studied with an air of humility, an open heart, and a desire to enter into communion with the God. The Vatican II document Dei Verbum tells us that God is truly the author of the sacred scriptures, but that the human authors are also fully authors.[1] The bible also tells us that the scriptures are *'God breathed' (cf. 2 Tim 3:16).* Thus we should seek the Holy Spirit when studying so that he can teach our hearts. *The seed of God's Word needs to find our hearts a place of good soil where it can produce a harvest. (cf. Mt 13:8)*

Meditations and scripture readings

If you are using this workbook as an 11-week (or longer) programme then you will find the scripture readings at the end of each chapter useful.

The meditations are there to be memorised if you can. Treat them as a medical prescription that needs to be taken 5 times a day (at meals). Whether you commit them to memory or not they will have an impact on you. Daily meditation on God's Word is vital for you to grow in your relationship with God.

'Prayerful reading of scripture, and the consequent reform of life, is the secret to the constant renewal of the Church.' Pope Benedict XVI.[2]

'If this practice (prayerful meditation on the scriptures) is promoted with efficacy, I am convinced that it will produce a new spiritual springtime in the Church.'

Pope Benedict XVI.[3]

The scripture readings are like a small meal. Please read them carefully and allow God to speak to your heart as you digest the content. None of us would eat quickly through a feast; we would eat slowly and savour the flavour. We need to treat God's Word the same way. Savour it, eat slowly; enjoy it. Let God converse with us while we eat:-

'We speak to God when we pray; we listen to him when we read the divine oracles.'[4]

Commitment

This is vital. You need to be committed to a daily time studying and praying the scriptures. Set aside sufficient time each day to prayerfully read the scriptures and take time out to meditate on the short lines. You need to set time aside to read the various chapters with elements for you to fill in. If you can do this then you will be greatly blessed as I was when first learning this topic. It may mean leaving the television off, cutting back on some socialising, or changing a daily habit. It may be a temporary change, but God may have other plans and it is a wise person who remains open to God's plan for their life.

Resources

I have included some of the main resources at the back of the course book. However, a lot of the teaching has come through perseverance in reading the scriptures, attending conferences, various retreats, and a wide range of reading. This book contains the fruit of 21 years of research, study and prayer.

CD's

All of the teachings in this course book are available on cd. It is not essential to have them. The book contains a lot of the information, but the cd's will give you added extras and something of a guide through the ancient world of blood covenants. It is a world which can have something of a mystery about it because the language is so different to ours. However, to understand the sacred scriptures it helps a great deal to study covenants.

A prayer

Before you start studying please take a short time of silence. For a few minutes listen to God and open yourself up to the Holy Spirit. Pray the Veni Creator below to help you.

Veni Creator

Come, Holy Spirit, Creator blest,
and in our souls take up Thy rest;
come with Thy grace and heavenly aid
to fill the hearts which Thou hast made
O comforter, to Thee we cry,
O heavenly gift of God Most High,
O fount of life and fire of love,
and sweet anointing from above.
Thou in Thy sevenfold gifts are known;
Thou, finger of God's hand we own;
Thou, promise of the Father, Thou
Who dost the tongue with power imbue.
Kindle our senses from above,
and make our hearts o'erflow with love;
with patience firm and virtue high
the weakness of our flesh supply.
Far from us drive the foe we dread,
and grant us Thy peace instead;
so shall we not, with Thee for guide,
turn from the path of life aside.
Oh, may Thy grace on us bestow
the Father and the Son to know;
and Thee, through endless times confessed,
of both the eternal Spirit blest.
Now to the Father and the Son,
Who rose from death, be glory given,
with Thou, O Holy Comforter,
henceforth by all in earth and heaven.
Amen.

Beginning to study

Read Hebrews 8:1-13. How many times is the word Covenant used? _______

From this scripture it is clear that God is referring to at least two covenants, the old covenant and the new covenant. We may be more familiar with the words 'old testament/new testament' but the word 'covenant' is more frequently used in the bible.

What is a covenant? In Hebrew the word is:-

'Berit'

Which means:-

"To cut where blood flows."

This is a literal translation which may be a little confusing. The bible in English is a translation from Hebrew and Greek with small elements of other languages. Occasionally the workbook will show the original Hebrew words in anglicised letters with a literal translation.

If we can grasp the meaning of a covenant the scriptures will become more accessible to us.

Covenant

An agreement to "cut a covenant by the shedding of blood

and walking between the pieces of flesh.

A blood covenant between two parties is the closest, the most enduring, the most solemn

and the most sacred of all contracts. It absolutely cannot be broken.[5]

There are several types of covenant but the most common type in the bible is blood covenant. The first blood covenant established in the bible is between two people:-

Write out Genesis 2:24.

____

____

This is the definition of the marriage covenant. Marriage is a blood covenant established, originally, between two people, male and female, man and woman.

Go to the last book of your bible, read Revelation 19:7 and write it below.

____

____

Then read Revelation 22:17. The first five words refer to the Holy Spirit and the Bride of Christ who is the Church. Write those five words below.

____

The bible begins and ends with marriage. This is also the approach we need to apply to our relationship with God. Some people can relate to God as a distant friend who is handy in times of trial. For others he is a close friend to visit once or twice a week. For those who really want to take their relationship with God seriously he is a fiancé to spend a great deal of time with who they plan on marrying one day.

This course will show you how to progress through the Old Covenant into the New Covenant of God's plan to lead you into a depth of intimacy in your relationship with God that is truly breathtaking.

1. The Marriage Covenant

As explained in the introduction, the bible is about covenants. Most regular churchgoers understand the word 'covenant' to mean a commitment to support the church financially. However, this is not the true meaning of the word. The original meaning was more to do with the relationship between people. Two tribes or two nations would have a covenant agreement. Two people can also have a covenant agreement. The term 'blood brothers' comes from a covenant agreement whereby two men want to make a specific commitment to one another to the degree that they cut their hands, mix blood, and make a 'vow'.

This chapter will be focussing on the covenant between a man and woman, the marriage covenant. In order to understand a little more about this covenant we need to examine some of the aspects of the marriage ceremony.

I was told a story of a priest giving a sermon at a marriage ceremony. He had been a priest for many years and went through a list of how many thousands of baptisms he had performed; how many teenagers he had confirmed with permission from the Bishop; how many first holy communions he had distributed; the vast number of confessions he had heard. Then he declared, 'I have never married anybody'.

As you read further you will understand this statement.

When I teach on this topic I usually ask the question 'Where do you think marriages take place?' Most people point to the venue where the wedding ceremony occurred; for Christians this would be a church. Others may say a hotel, ship, park, castle, beach, or some other location. However, although the venues described are where we take part in the wedding ceremony they are not where we get 'married'. To help with this please write down from a dictionary the definition of marriage (look up 'marry'):-

____

Read Genesis 2:24.

The definition of marriage is 'to join together'. This joining does not take place in a public ceremony. What takes place in a church or other venue is:-

1. Gathering of witnesses
2. Exchange of vows (until death do us part!)
3. Signing of a register.
4. Final statement by the officiating person (for Catholics this would be a priest). Ie. 'I now pronounce you man and wife'.

Although all of this belongs to the wedding ceremony, none of it is the marriage. To marry means 'to join together' and at no point in the above examples are two joined together as one. The terminology may imply a joining together, but until the man and woman are joined together they are not 'married'.

What takes place in church is known as the 'sacramental liturgy' and the 'marriage contract', as described by Pope John Paul II in the Theology of the Body.[6] He also declares that until the marriage is consummated on the wedding night 'the marriage is not yet constituted in its full reality'.[7]

The marriage takes place when the happy couple engage in sexual intercourse for the first time. This is why the Catholic Church discourages sex before marriage. This is like saying with your body that you are getting married (two becoming one) but in reality there is no commitment to that union.

The sacramental liturgy with the priest and witnesses takes place in the Church. The priest blesses the marriage and presides over the liturgy.[8]

MARRIAGE TO GOD

Marriage is a blood covenant that is consummated on the wedding night. In a sacramental sense the husband and wife administer the sacrament of marriage to one another.[9]

A promise of marriage is to give your life, your health, your wealth, your happiness, forever, until death do us part. All resources are shared. If one party has debt and other has credit, the credit clears the debt. Marital partners should sacrifice themselves to restore their spouse: "For better or for worse; for richer or for poorer; in sickness and in health, till death do us part."

Write out Ephesians 5:23 and 5:32

____

____

A ritual currently spreading across the Catholic Church in Europe as part of the marriage ceremony is the husband and wife both take hold of the same cross and the priest says to each 'your spouse is your cross'.[10] This is having a profound affect on marriages.

BETROTHAL

Before we get married we enter into an engagement, known as a betrothal.

What does Hosea 2:21 say about God's betrothal/espousal to you (In some translations like the RSV it will be verse 19)?

____

____

When you were baptised and subsequently confirmed you were betrothed to Jesus Christ.

What does Jesus say to his disciples (us) in the Gospel of John 14:1-3?

____

____

This statement reflects part of a Jewish betrothal ceremony. When Jesus was speaking these words to His disciples at the last supper He was betrothing them to Himself. It may have been very hard for them to comprehend what was taking place but they would have understood after he sent the Holy Spirit. These are the words that Joseph would have spoken to Mary when they were betrothed. Joseph would then return to his father's house and prepare a room for Mary, the bridal chamber. Mary would go to her mother and be prepared for her wedding. The preparation could take over a year but when they are both ready they can be married and go to the bridal chamber to consummate the marriage. As we know this did not take place with Joseph and Mary. Even though they lived together as husband and wife there was no physical consummation. The same applies to our relationship with God where the consummation is purely spiritual. Our union with God is spiritual.

Betrothal

Hebrew – Kiddushim

Comes from the Hebrew word

Kadosh - Holy

This is because the word 'kiddushim' means 'sanctified' and carries the idea that the wife is now sanctified (dedicated or set apart) for her husband. Just as 'holy' means set apart. Although tradition specifies the woman as being sanctified the Hebrew word 'Kiddushim' is masculine, thus applying to the man. It is pointing us towards Christ. He is the 'Holy One'. The plurality ('im' at the end of a Hebrew word makes it plural) is because it applies to the Trinity. Our holiness is because of Christ. If we want union with him we must also be holy. We should desire this union and holiness.

Genesis 2:24 talks of man who leaves his father and mother and cleaves to his wife and the two become one flesh. This scripture is also speaking of Jesus Christ who left his Father in heaven, then left his mother at the wedding feast of Cana.

Read John 2:4. What does Jesus say to his mother?

____

____

The 'hour' that Jesus is referring to is that of his passion, death and resurrection. Jesus leaves his mother at this point and the wedding feast narrative concludes with the statement in verse 11.

What does this verse say about his disciples?

____

The Greek word for believe is:-

Pisteuo

To believe, entrust.

From pistis

To adhere to, rely on.

It could be said that at this point Jesus clings to his wife, the Church, represented by the disciples, and the two become one flesh, the body of Christ.

Marriage is a covenant relationship echoing the relationship that God has with His people. Within marriage there is an intimacy between husband and wife that is exclusive to that relationship. God wants to have a similar but spiritual intimacy with all who choose to walk in His ways. God uses the same language about our relationship with Him that would be used within the context of the sexual union of husband and wife.

Read Genesis 4:1 and write it below:-

____

____

Jeremiah 9:22,23 reads:-

'Thus says the LORD: Let not the wise man glory in his wisdom, nor the strong man glory in his strength, nor the rich man glory in his riches; But rather, let him who glories, glory in this, that in his prudence he <u>knows</u> me.'

The Hebrew word for '*relations*,' or '*sexual intercourse*' and that for '*knows*' are the same:-

Yada – 'to know'.

What does Isaiah 54:5 say regarding God as husband?

____

What does Hebrews 8:11 say regarding the consequences of the new and everlasting covenant bearing in mind the use of the word 'know'?

____

God reveals himself to us using the idea of friendship (John 15:15, 'I have called you friends) but He wants us to be his bride. The bible shows us how God leads his people gradually, gently and lovingly from being his spiritual friends to his spiritual lovers; His spouse.

MARRIAGE

A couple getting married enter into the marriage contract at the church and receive the sacrament of marriage. They are both ministers of this sacrament through firstly their words, then later via their actions. In this sense the marriage sacrament is like the Eucharist:-

First the priest speaks the words through which Christ transforms the bread and wine into flesh and blood.[11] Then the priest presents the flesh and blood to us for consumption.

The priest and the couple speak the words through which Christ blesses the marriage sacrament. Then the man and woman administer the sacrament of marriage to one another in sexual union.[12]

Now that we understand this principle we can look at some of the symbols used throughout the wedding ceremony. The wedding rings, the cake; the bridal gown, wedding gifts and guests. The latter are also known as witnesses. Finally the wedding meal at which there is wine and a memorial/wedding meal. All of these have an important symbolic meaning as well as the traditional role they play.

THE WEDDING RING

This is the physical sign of the covenant, known in ancient times as the covenant scar. The primary purpose of the wedding ring is as a sign of the covenant to show publicly that the person wearing the ring has a covenant relationship with another person and thus is not free to do as they please. They belong to somebody else by their own free choice.

The ring is usually placed on the third finger of left hand; it was once believed that a vein on that finger ran to the heart, the ring was being placed on the heart and the heart was pumping life into the marriage.[13] This vein is called 'Vena Amoris' (Latin for 'vein of love'). In ancient times instead of using a ring a scar was made on the thumb as a permanent sign of the covenant. In the scriptures this is called the 'seal' of the covenant; or the sign, token, or testimony. It is the physical sign that you are in covenant with somebody else.[14]

Here are some scriptures with signs of the covenant. Write down the sign/seal/token/mark:-

*Genesis 4:15.*____

*Genesis 9:13*____

*Genesis 17:11*____

*Exodus 31:16, 17*____

*2 Chronicles 7:18*____

2 Corinthians 1:22 ____

Ephesians 1:13 ____

NAME CHANGE

If a person changes their name it is a sign that they are changing their whole identity. This is what takes place when a person is baptised. Getting married means laying your life down so that you are living a new life for somebody else. Up to the point of marriage you have lived for yourself, now you are going to live for somebody else whom you love enough to lay your life down for.

What does Romans 14:8 say about living and dying with regard to our relationship with the Lord Jesus?

____

____

WITNESSES

Every covenant needs witnesses and God has witnesses Himself. His disciples bear witness to Him and His covenant with the Church. The witnesses see the covenant being consummated and then bear witness to what they have seen.

Read John 19:26, 27 which recounts the beloved disciple and the mother of Jesus witnessing the death of Jesus. What does Jesus say to them?

____

____

St John is telling us that we are the beloved disciple and bear witness to the death of Jesus through our faith in the power of his resurrection. Your marriage relationship to God bears witness against the world and for the kingdom of God. It is a visible testimony of the love of Christ for his Church and shows that there is a power greater than sin, greater than evil; the power of love.

Read the first letter of St John 4:12. How does God's love come to perfection in us?

____

VOWS/PROMISES

These are the covenant terms. All agreements have terms, what are known as promises and curses. The bible contains all the covenant terms for our relationship with God.

Read 2 Corinthian 1:20. What does it say about the promises of God?

CLOTHING

No doubt the bride will want to buy a beautiful dress. While the groom and his entourage will hire/buy morning suits or something of a similar persuasion. This is what people of ancient times would have done; worn their finest clothing to show their 'colours'. You don't enter into a covenant relationship dressed in rags.

Read Matthew 22:1-13 paying attention to verse 12. What happens to the man in verses 12 and 13?

This man would have been given a wedding suit to put on when he arrived.[15] To stay at the feast without the garment on would be to dishonour the 'king'. This is like the kingdom of heaven. God gives each of us all the graces we need to enter into heavenly glory. If we refuse them and try to enter wearing the filthy rags of our own deeds (eg, 'I am a good person', 'I don't hurt anybody', etc), we will be thrown out. Nobody is worthy of heaven on their own merit. It is all about the grace of God.

Luke 15:22 the return of the Prodigal Son:-

"His son said to him, 'Father, I have sinned against heaven and against you; I no longer deserve to be called your son.' But his father ordered his servants, 'Quickly bring the finest robe and put it on him; put a ring on his finger and sandals on his feet."

The father puts his finest robe on the prodigal son. This is the Father's own robe and manifests his glory. When a person returns to relationship with God he puts his glory on them and clothes them in grace.

EXCHANGE OF GIFTS

Nobody brings their worst gift to a wedding ceremony; they will usually select something special. We should also bring our best gifts to church to enable the building up of God's kingdom on earth.

Read John 17:24. Who is the gift of God to Jesus?

What we bring into church on a Sunday morning is our response!

When a married couple make love on the wedding night they are offering themselves to their spouse as a gift. They are also receiving from their spouse the gift of themselves, fully, without reserve. The act of sexual intercourse is a mutual self-giving. They give the best they have – self, no reserve, given fully. That is what it means to make love.

THE WEDDING FEAST

This is known as the covenant meal. All who partake in the covenant and witness it are invited to share. It is a remembrance and a celebration of that which has taken place. As Christians this is why Jesus celebrated the last supper with his disciples and told us:-

'Do this in remembrance of me' (cf. 1 Cor. 11:24).

WEDDING CAKE

The cake symbolises the body. The cutting of the cake is symbolic of cutting covenant. Eating the cake is symbolic of the sexual union. Marriage does not happen until the sexual union is completed. The sexual union is the sacrament of marriage that the husband and wife minister to one another. They are both ministers of the sacrament. The interesting thing is that every time the couple make love they are renewing their marriage vows. Every time they have sexual intercourse they are ministering the sacrament of marriage to one another. This is total, mutual self-giving.

WINE (CHAMPAGNE)

This symbolises blood. The couple give it to one another. This is a sign that they are willing to lay their life down for the person they are marrying. One gives the wine to the other, a full offering of their very life blood. They fully receive the gift and offer their own blood to their spouse. A foreshadowing of the marital union when the marriage is consummated. It is also a sign of the sacrifice that is necessary in order for marriage to work. If there is no sacrifice the marriage will struggle as both parties will pull towards themselves. If there is mutual sacrificial self-giving the couple will lean towards one another in true love

(1 Cor 13:5 'love does not insist on its own way).

SOME COVENANT FACTS

EUROPE'S OLDEST COVENANT

This is between England and Portugal (700 years old). In 1386 both nations signed the Treaty of Windsor, the oldest alliance in Europe still in force. The Anglo-Portuguese Alliance[1] was renewed in 1386[2] with the Treaty of Windsor[3] and the marriage of King John I of Portugal[4] (House of Aviz[5]) with Philippa of Lancaster[6], daughter of John of Gaunt[7].[16]

THE BUGANDA TRIBE

When I was in Uganda in 2010 I was told of a tribe that still maintains a blood covenant ritual. If two men in this tribe want to make their friendship permanent they will take a coffee bean and break it open. Within the bean are two seeds. Each man will take a seed, cut his side near the ribcage, immerse the seed in his side so that it is soaked in blood, and offer the seed to his friend. Each of the men receives the blood covered seed from his friend and eats it so that the seed and his friend's blood are inside him.

From this time onwards these two men are blood brothers in a very real sense. It is taken so seriously within the tribe that the father's of the men will change their inheritance. If one of the men has two sons, he will now treat this son's friend as another son and include him in the family inheritance so instead of having two sons he has three.

JUDAISM

Here are a few insights from the Jewish wedding ceremony.[17]

The Jewish marriage certificate is called a **Ketubah** which is signed at the start of the ceremony. The end of the ceremony is marked by the groom breaking a wine glass which symbolizes the destruction of Jerusalem and the fragility of marriage.

Jewish couples marry under a banner called a **Huppah**, a cloth canopy supported by four poles. In some places a prayer shawl is held over the couple. This symbolizes the couples new home. It means that their home is held together by prayer which flows from God's Word.

In ancient Israel when the married couple had finished with the ceremony they would go to the bridal chamber to consummate the marriage. This would take place behind a veil but witnessed by both sets of in-laws. When the marriage had been consummated they would take the sheet stained with blood from the breaking of the bride's hymen and hang it out of a prominent window as a testimony.

---

1. http://en.wikipedia.org/wiki/Anglo-Portuguese_Alliance

2. http://en.wikipedia.org/wiki/1386

3. http://en.wikipedia.org/wiki/Windsor,_Berkshire

4. http://en.wikipedia.org/wiki/John_I_of_Portugal

5. http://en.wikipedia.org/wiki/House_of_Aviz

6. http://en.wikipedia.org/wiki/Philippa_of_Lancaster

7. http://en.wikipedia.org/wiki/John_of_Gaunt

In Goa the bride keeps the veil over her face until she reads the terms of the marriage covenant, then the veil is lifted. This comes from Judaism and is a reflection of what the above scripture says. The veil is not lifted until the bride enters into the covenant relationship.

The wedding veil – 2Cor 3:12-18

"Therefore, since we have such hope, we act very boldly and not like Moses, who put a veil over his face so that the Israelites could not look intently at the cessation of what was fading .... To this day, in fact, whenever Moses is read, a veil lies over their hearts, but whenever a person turns to the Lord the veil is removed. Now the Lord is the Spirit, and where the Spirit of the Lord is, there is freedom. All of us, gazing with unveiled face on the glory of the Lord, are being transformed into the same image from glory to glory, as from the Lord who is the Spirit."

There is a veil over the heart of those who read the scripture without recognising that Jesus is Lord. It does not make sense to them. When a person turns to Jesus that veil is lifted, the covenant makes sense, and salvation is theirs. This particularly applies to the Jews who, although they are still the people of God, do not recognise that Jesus is the Messiah. God has put a veil over their heart for his purpose just as described in the above scripture.

WHY BLOOD?

There seems to be quite a focus on blood in the bible and consequently in this bible study. There is a reason for this but it may not really become apparent until one of the latter chapters. In the meantime here are a few points for consideration:-

LIFE IS IN THE BLOOD

Every disease is a disease of the blood. White cells carry the immunity around the body via blood. All sexually transmitted diseases are transmitted via blood including HIV/AIDS. A married couple who remain faithful to one another, no matter how often they engage in sexual relations, will never 'infect' one another.

BLOOD CLEANSES

Blood is said to be the most powerful cleansing agent.

According to 1 John 1:7 what does the blood of Jesus do?

____

BLOOD MEANS LIFE

When a person gets married and enters into the marital blood covenant they are giving their entire self, without reserve, to another. They cannot do that, change their mind and then do it to somebody else. This is why the Catholic Church does not accept divorce. The teaching on annulment means that the marriage did not happen for various reasons which are beyond the scope of this study.

BLOOD

Is one reason that God does not approve of pre-marital (non-marital) sex, or extra-marital sex (adultery).

Read Deuteronomy 22:13-22. What is the penalty for pre-marital (non-marital) sex?

____

This can be seen in the light of the modern age whereby a couple who engage in sex before marriage are committing a mortal sin. They separate themselves from the life of God and experience a spiritual death. This can be healed through confession and a firm amendment of life.

BLOOD IS SACRED

Write out Leviticus 17:11:-

____

DAILY MEDITATIONS AND READINGS
These are given if you are studying this course book on a weekly basis, or with the cd set that can accompany the book. Otherwise they can be used for additional study or spiritual reading (Lectio Divina).

Meditations Readings
Day one: Song of songs 2:16 Ephesians 1:17-21
Day two: Songs of Songs 1:2 Ephesians 3:14-21
Day three: Songs of Songs 1:4 Ephesians 5:21-33
Day four: Revelation 19:7 Hosea 2:16-25
Day five: Ephesians 5:26 Psalm 45
Day six: John 14:3 Isaiah 62
Day seven: Wisdom 8:2 Ecclesiasticus 15

Everlasting Covenant with God.

(Write your name in the blanks)

For God so loved __________ that he gave his only Son, so that if __________ believes in him they may not perish but might have eternal life.

John 3:16

For I know well the plans I have in mind for ______________, says the LORD, plans for ________________ welfare, not for woe! plans to give __________ a future full of hope.

Jeremiah 29:11

Blessed be the God and Father of our Lord Jesus Christ, who has blessed ____________ in Christ with every spiritual blessing in the heavens.

Ephesians 1:3

See what love the Father has bestowed on ___________ that ________ may be called a child of God. And so__________ is.

1 John 3:1

God chose ________________ in him, before the foundation of the world, to be holy and without blemish before him.

Ephesians 1:4

God knew _________________ before _________________ was formed in the womb.

Jeremiah 1:5

Before _______________ has spoken a word God knows it because he knows my thoughts from afar.

Psalm 139:2,4

Every one of_______________ actions is known: They are written in God's book of life and all my days are shaped.

Psalm 139:16

For__________________ is his handiwork, created in Christ Jesus for the good works that God has prepared in advance, that __________________ should live in them

Ephesians 2:10

(The Saints) do not cease praying for _______________ and asking that you may be filled with the knowledge of his will through all spiritual wisdom and understanding

Colossians 1:9

Jesus is always able to save _______________ who approaches God through him, since he lives forever to make intercession for them.

2. The Nine Steps of a Hebrew Blood Covenant Ritual

The nine steps are how two Hebrews or two tribes in ancient times would have entered into a blood covenant. The following nine steps are still in use today in some cultures and religions.

From each tribe the best two people are chosen. These may be the mightiest warriors, the chiefs or the kings. In 1 Samuel 17 a battle scene is shown which is not the cutting of a covenant but it serves as an example. The outcome of the battle will be one nation serving the other. Two men must fight each other; the first is in:

1 Samuel 17:4. Name and describe him:-

____

The other warrior is in 1 Samuel 17:37. How does he plan on winning the victory?

____

All the people involved, including witnesses, wear the very best regalia that they have, as would the two cutting the covenant. If they are warriors they wear full battle dress. These are called the 'mediators' of the covenant. If the covenant is broken they pay the price which usually means one of them would have to die. (It is wise for a small, weak tribe to cut covenant with a powerful one.) Here are the nine steps:-

Take off robe and exchange. Represents status, royalty.

Take off belt and exchange.

Cut covenant

Raise right arms, slash hands and mix blood.

Exchange names (and gifts)

Make a permanent scar

Give the terms of covenant, blessings and curses

Eat a meal together – memorial meal

Plant a memorial tree [18]

The nine steps with more detail:-

1. EXCHANGE OF ROBES

The robe represents your position in society, your very person; by giving your robe to another person you are giving your total being, your status. It is an outward sign of an inward reality. The sacraments are like this (cf. CCC 774). By swapping cloaks the mediators are pledging their whole life to one another.[19] It is a sign of holiness. In the Bible the robe is also referred to as a cloak or mantle.

Read 1 Samuel 18:4. Who are the two pledging allegiance to one another?

____

In 1 Kings 19:19 what does Elijah do?

____

In Luke 15:22 what does the Father order the servants to do?

____

2. BELT

This is exchanged. This is not for holding up trousers, it holds weapons. By exchanging the belt I am pledging support and protection, all my strength and ability to fight; I will fight with you, I will defend you.[20]

Read Ephesians 6:10. What is the belt Christians wear?

____

The belt was used by Roman soldiers to tie loose garments so the soldiers would not trip up whilst in battle. The belt of truth prevents us from tripping over lies.

3. CUT COVENANT

Get the very best sheep, set aside, nurtured, unblemished (this is usually considered to be a family pet!). It is split down the middle so blood flows (The Hebrew word for covenant, 'Berit', means to cut where blood flows). The animal is a substitute for us. We stand in the carcass, in the blood. Beginning back to back we walk in a figure of eight so that we finish face to face. As we walk we say, whilst pointing at the carcass "God do this to me if I break this most solemn of covenants". We're dying to self, giving up the right to our own life, beginning a new walk with our covenant partner. [21]

What does Jeremiah 34:18 say about the men who break the covenant?

____

4. RAISE RIGHT ARM

We cut the palm of the hand. Our blood flows. We join hands and mix blood swearing allegiance to the covenant.[22] As the blood mixes our lives are intermingling because the life of the creature is in the blood. The old nature is taken off and we put on our new nature. We are becoming 'one'. The right hand is the weapon hand. By doing this we are declaring to one another, 'I'm laying down my weapons and I'll never fight you again; your battles are my battles, and vice versa.'

We raise our right arm if we need to take a solemn vow in a court of law.

This is where we get the origin of the idea of blood brothers and the traditional handshake.

What does 2 Corinthian 5:17 say about us being a new creation in Christ?

____

____

5. Exchange names

A new identity comes with a new name. In the Bible the word for name, 'shem' can mean 'character, mission, reputation, identity'. Receiving a new name means the old name has died and you have taken on a new identity, new mission; a new character. This can happen at Baptism, Confirmation, Marriage or when a man or woman enters into religious life. Jesus said of his name;

"If you declare me before men, I will remember your name before my Father in Heaven" (Mt 10:32, 33)
EXCHANGE GIFTS

Give the best you have got. Tithing is a sign of covenant relationship; you give the first 10% of your income. Farmers give the first fruits of their produce. Nobody can afford this; it must be an act of faith, a belief in God's providence. Malachi 3 is a classic scripture passage with regards to tithing.

Before the Reformation when the Catholic Church was the only Church in this nation, it was a legal requirement to tithe. Many villages had a

Tithe Barn where the tithed produce was stored.[23]

When Henry VIII reformed/destroyed the church the tithe was no longer given to 'God' but was taken by the state.[24] Since then God has received what is known as the 'gleanings' at the traditional autumn harvest festival. The gleanings are the scraps that are left after the harvest has been gathered in.

Read Leviticus 19:9, 10. Who are the gleanings left for?

____

Read Deuteronomy 26:12-14. What does the Word of God call the tithe in verse 13 and who is the tithe given to?

____

At Baptism we are given a name and we become 'Christian", taking Jesus' name. At confirmation the Church encourages us to get involved in the mission of the church, so we are not just being sealed with the Holy Spirit, we choose a new name, hence a new identity, and supposedly beginning a new life as a result of receiving our mission in life. Baptism fulfils circumcision because when a man is circumcised they are entering into the covenant. Since the resurrection of Jesus men enter into the covenant via baptism. Confirmation could be said to fulfil the Jewish Bar/Bat Mitzvah because it is when a person chooses the covenant for themselves and they partake in the mission of the Church. Just as a Jewish boy or girl as part of their bar/bat mitzvah they can read from the Torah and are considered to be mature.[25]

Jews in the bible are named in accordance with their mission in life or their character followed by their father's first name.

Jesus was called Yeshuah bar Yoseph.

Jesus son of Joseph (so it was thought!).

He was also called Yeshuah bar Elohim

(Jesus, Son of God)

The name Jesus means 'God saves'

6. MAKE SCAR

We make a circular wound on the thumb and rub salt into it to make a personal, visible testimony. This is probably where we get the phrase 'rub salt into the wound'. It is a covenant statement. The visible scar is known as the seal and the guarantee of the covenant.[26] It has a similar meaning to a wedding ring but it cannot be removed.

In Romans 4:11 what is the seal of the Old Covenant?

____

In Ephesians 1:13 what is the seal of the New Covenant?

____

Copy out Ephesians 4:30?

____

The first instalment is the deposit guaranteeing the fullness of blessings (cf. CCC 655).

7. DECLARE THE COVENANT TERMS

"All my assets, all my money, my property, possessions are all yours. If I die my children are yours by adoption, my liabilities and debts are yours".[27] There are blessings for keeping the covenant; there are curses for breaking it. In the bible the blessings are associated with life, the curses with death.

Read Deuteronomy 28:1-14. How many times is the word 'blessing' used?

____

8. MEMORIAL MEAL

Bread (represents our flesh) and wine (blood of the grape represents our blood).[28] We break the bread in two and feed it to each other saying, "This is my body that I feed to you." The same is done with the wine which is symbolic of my blood. At the last supper/Mass Jesus gives us literally his flesh and blood. It is not symbolic.

Copy out John 6:53

____

____

The 'Breaking of Bread' is the covenant meal

Instituted by Christ.

Now known as The Holy Mass.[29]

9. PLANT A MEMORIAL TREE

A tree is planted and sprinkled with the blood of the animal that was slain using a hyssop stick which has water in the stem. The blood is mixed with water from the stem so that the blood and water testify to the covenant.[30]

Copy out John 19:34

____

____

CONCLUSION OF THE COVENANT

Now we are friends – 'I have called you friends.' (John 15:12-14)

The ancient understanding of covenant friendship is that you would lay down your life for your friends. You did not call a person a friend unless you had a covenant relationship with them. Jesus calls us his friends because we are in covenant with Him.

Our children are included in the covenant because they are in our loins. We are obliged to teach them the covenant and at a certain age they can accept or reject the covenant.

BAR/BAT MITZVAH

All Hebrew boys are circumcised after 8 days in order that the may receive the blessings of the covenant. When they reach a certain age (12 for girls, 13 for boys) they undergo a ritual where they become a son/daughter of the commandment. This is also known as the bar/bat mitzvah.[31]

Bar = son

Bat = daughter

Mitzvah = commandment

This is the event at which they 'come of age' or are 'mature' because they can read from the Torah for the first time and they choose to follow the ways of God revealed in Judaism.

They accept or reject the covenant.

The parallel for Catholics is Confirmation.

However, there is no choice over circumcision/baptism as this is the responsibility of the parent or guardian.

Daily meditations and readings:-
(Pay particular attention to all usage of the word 'covenant')
Meditations Readings
Day one: Jeremiah 31:33 Colossians 2
Day two: Isaiah 61:8 Sirach 17
Day three: Ezekiel 16:62 Hebrews 8
Day four: Psalm 105:8 Matthew 26:20-29
Day five: Genesis 6:18 Acts 3
Day six: Matthew 26:28 2 Corinthians 3
Day seven: 1 Corinthian 10:21 Jeremiah 33

3. In the Beginning

God reveals Himself from the very first words of the bible. Our God is one of revelation who reveals Himself to us in order that we may seek and find Him.[32] God reveals Himself through His Word in much the same way as we reveal ourselves when we speak.

Write down Genesis 1:1:-

____

____

In the first sentence of the bible the Blessed Trinity are revealed, but in order to discover the Trinity we need to access the rest of the scriptures and the Creed. Go to the last book of the bible, the book of Revelation, also known as Apocalypse.

What does Jesus call himself in chapter 22 verse 13?

____

The Bible begins with the words 'in the beginning' and virtually ends with Jesus declaring 'I am the beginning'. Hence we might be able to read it as, 'In Jesus, God created the heavens and the earth'.

Read St Paul's letter to the Colossians 1:16. What was created in Christ?

____

____

The next words in Genesis are 'God created' which is pointing to the Father as does the Creed:-
'I believe in One God, the Father, the Almighty, Creator of heaven and earth'
Finally we have the revelation of the Holy Spirit,
'A mighty wind swept over the waters'.
Hebrew uses the following words for 'mighty wind'.

'Ruach Elohim'

Ruach = Wind, Spirit, Breath

Elohim = God.

Thus:-'The Spirit of God'

Hence in Genesis 1:1,2 we have the revelation of God as Father, Son and Holy Spirit, though that would not be known unless we read all the way to the end of the bible and God revealed it to us.

After God has created the heavens and the earth, what is the next thing God creates and what does he call it?
The answer is in Genesis 1:3?

____

The Hebrew word for day is 'yom'. It can also be translated 'eternity'. Thus the self revelation of God's nature as light can be called 'eternity'. The light is eternal life; our eternal life is going to be spent in eternal light, eternal day.

God's word is creative. He says "Let there be..." and what he says exists. It is God's creation. Everything that God creates is 'good' and reflects His glory. The first thing that God speaks into being is the divine light, his self revelation. This is not the sun which is created in verse 16 (the greater light to mark the day), this is the self revelation of God's glory.

Turn to the first letter of Saint John, chapter 1 verse 5 which is near the back of your bible. What word does John use to describe God?

____

As God speaks he reveals himself, his glory, his nature. This is so that the creatures he is making can know him and give him the glory due to him.[33]

Take a look at the order in which God creates.

Day one Let there be light

Day four Let there be lights in the sky.

Day two Let there be a dome in the middle of the waters

Day five Let the water teem with an abundance of living creatures

Day three Let the earth bring forth vegetation

Day six Let the earth bring forth all kinds of living creatures

First God creates the various environments; then he creates the living creatures to populate those environments.

In Genesis 1:26 God's language changes; rather than saying 'let there be' write down what God says regarding the creation of man:-

____

____

Some commentators state the 'us' in this line refers to God and the heavenly court, the angels. However, angels do not have creative powers. They are ministering spirits sent to serve (see Hebrews 1). The 'us' refers to the three persons of the Trinity. All of the action in creation is the action of the Blessed Trinity. None of them work in isolation; they work in perfect unity.[34]

Out of everything that has been created only mankind has been created 'in his image'; this makes humanity unique amongst the whole of creation.

GOD'S BLESSING

God gives man 'dominion' which means 'To rule, to dominate'. Thus God has created everything and now hands it all over to man (man in Hebrew is Adam) which once again shows God's self-giving nature. This action makes Adam the king of the world, the great high priest, the world ruler, the mediator of the covenant. Everything that God has made in the physical realm is under Adam's dominion (cf. Ps. 8).

What blessing does God give to mankind in Genesis 1:28?

____

____

Man's fruitfulness and dominion are a sign of his blessedness in the sight of God. Adam dominates the world out of love, not out of fear, sin, hate, anger, or any other other sinful expression. At this stage in creation Adam is a man of love and his rule is one of love. There is perfect harmony in Eden because man and creation are in harmony with God.[35]

The story of creation has another account beginning in Genesis 2. There are no contradictions between the two accounts, just a different emphasis.

Genesis 2:7 describes God creating man. Write out the scripture:-

____

____

There are three phrases to ponder in respect of the creation of man:-

Clay of the ground - flesh

Breath of life – Spirit

Living being – soul

The Hebrew for breath in this circumstance is:-

neshemah

A difference between ruach and neshemah is that at the heart of the word neshemah is the word 'shem' which means name. This is the word that brings life to man, it gives him his character, identity, reputation and his mission in life (shem means all of these). All this comes when man has the 'neshemah' of life within him.

THE COVENANT TERMS

Genesis 2:16, 17 God gives Adam, as the ruler of the earth, the mediator, and the High Priest, the covenant terms. What are they?

____

____

Adam has free access to the tree of life and every other tree in the Garden of Eden. There is but one tree that he cannot eat the fruit from or he will suffer the one, sole consequence – death. The tree of the knowledge of good and evil bears fruit that kills.

Man is alone among the animals and to reveal this to man God brings all the animals to him inviting him to name the animals. The naming of the animals is a sign of Adam's ruling power. If God was the ruler he would name the animals, but as Adam is the ruler he does the naming. He relies on God to bring the animals to him, but Adam has the power and authority to name them.

Name in Hebrew = 'shem'

'Shem' = Character, nature, mission in life.

As Adam gives each animal its name he gives each animal its character and its nature. However, man remains isolated.

What does Genesis 2:20 say about the condition of man?

____

Man needs to feel his isolation and his need before he can accept the gift that God wants to give him.

Write down Genesis 2:21, 22

____

____

In the same way that God took Eve from the side of Adam, the Church is born from the side of Jesus on the cross.[36]

The Marriage Covenant

God gives the woman to the man as a gift. Man receives the woman and offers himself to her in response to the gift. The best way to accept a gift is to offer a gift; this is the way a covenant works.

Read Genesis 2:24.

This is the definition of marriage. It is not about a certificate or a Registry Office; it is about man and woman, in the grace of God, giving mutually and exclusively to one another in the act of sexual intercourse. That is marriage; intimate union, two becoming one body.[37]

The fall

Prior to the fall humanity, in the persons of Adam and Eve was in a state of sanctifying grace. They were created in a state of holiness, in communion with God to such an extent that they could walk in the Garden of Eden in the presence of God. There was no fear, no disease, no sickness; no sin. Death had not entered into the world and our first parents were immortal. If Adam had not sinned he would still be alive today and there would not have been any sin, sickness, disease, famine, plagues, war, death, destruction or misery. Every person who had ever been born would still be alive and there would be plenty of food to go around. The world would be one land mass (Genesis 1:9) and would most beautifully reflect the glory of God. Everybody on earth would be in communion with God and be in a state of such explicit and perfect happiness. Sadly, this is not the case, but it will be one day when God restores all things.

Read Genesis 3:1-14

What does the serpent ask the woman in Genesis 3:1?

____

____

The serpent is the fallen angel known as Satan. He is the demon who was created in glory and beauty but also rejected God's plan for his life and fell to earth. Adam has dominion over the serpent but the serpent wants to change that.

Note that the serpent does not approach Adam, who received the Word of God directly from God. He approaches the woman!

What does Eve say to the serpent in Genesis 3:3? (The fruit in the middle of the garden)

____

____

Compare that with the original instruction given to Adam in Genesis 2:17. Write it below.

____

Eve did not fully understand the Word of God which allowed the serpent to deceive her. Deception is not the telling of a blatant lie. It can be part truthful and part falsehood; but it is intended to cause you to question what you have heard.

Read Genesis 3:4, 5.

The serpent is partly right. If Eve only touches the fruit she will not die. However, he is also deceiving because Adam and Eve are already like 'gods'. They are the world rulers. If Eve eats the fruit she will die, that is, she will not be like God.

Read Genesis 3:6 and describe the fruit that leads to death?

____

____

In the same scripture where was Adam when this was taking place and what did Eve do with the fruit she had taken and ate?

____

____

The first/original sin

God created an angel called Lucifer which means bearer of light.[38] He was created in beauty and perfection. Rather than choose to love God for all eternity he chose self and fell from the heights of heaven to earth. At that time he also lost his ministerial name (Lucifer) and was given a new name and new ministry – Satan which means accuser.

Satan had rebelled, in order to gain power on earth he had to get Adam to join his rebellion by disobeying God. As Adam knows the full terms of the covenant and is the high priest and mediator Satan does not approach him directly but goes to his wife first. Also, rather than speaking in plain language Satan uses trickery to confuse her and lead her into his rebellion. Thus Satan steals Adam's dominion, becomes the god of this world (1 John 5:19), and the accuser of the brethren (Job 1:6 and Revelation 12:10). This is the root cause for the world being in such a mess to this day.

The effects of original sin:

Shame – Lust – Fear – Death – Disease – Sickness – Pride – War – Famine – Plague – Lust – Immorality – Selfishness – Hate – Murder, etc.

Death was not God's plan; it was man reaching out for that which he had been expressly told not to. It is worth noting that God did not restrict man's access to the tree of life until after the fall and for a specific reason.

Read Wisdom 1:13 and write down what it says about God and death.

____

Rather than repenting, Adam accuses, as does Eve. The covenant curses come into effect; and at the same time the promise of a redeemer. God clothes the man and the woman in animal skins.

In Genesis 3:15 God makes a promise of victory. What is it?

____

____

With respect to the woman it should read:-

'She shall crush thy head, and thou shalt lie in wait for her heel'[39]

The 'she' is a reference to the mother of the redeemer. As a woman was a key player in the fall of humanity, so a woman has to be a key player in its restoration.

Situation

- God lost access to the earth which he had through Adam
- Satan has legal rights and becomes god of this world.
- Man is under a curse, the sin of Adam/original sin
- Because a man was a key figure in the fall, a man has to be the key figure in the redemption
- God needed a man of free will to accomplish this.

What does the Church say about Genesis? [40]

- God created everything "in its own substance" from nothing (ex nihilo) in the beginning. (Lateran IV; Vatican Council I) [41]
- Genesis does not contain purified myths. (Pontifical Biblical Commission 1909)
- Genesis contains real history – it contains an account of things that really happened (Pope Pius XII)
- Adam and Eve were real human beings – the first parents of all mankind (Pope Pius XII)
- The body of Eve was specially created from a portion of Adam's body.[42]
- According to a decision of the Bible Commission the literal historical sense is to be adhered to in regard to the formation of the first woman out of the first man.[43]
- Adam and eve were created upon an earthly paradise and would not have known death if they had remained obedient (Pope Pius XII)
- Original Sin is a flawed condition inherited from Adam and Eve (Council of Trent)
- After their disobedience of God, Adam and Eve were banished from the Garden of Eden. But the Second Person of the Trinity would subsequently pay the ransom for fallen man (Nicene Creed).

Daily meditations and readings:

Meditations Readings

Day one: Genesis 1:3 Deuteronomy 30:15-20

Day two: Genesis 2:7 Psalm 104

Day three: Genesis 1:28 John 14

Day four: Genesis 6:18 Song of Songs 8

Day five: Sirach 1:9 Psalm 112

Day six: Wisdom 7:7 Wisdom 8

Day seven: Genesis 4:26 John 17

4. Noah, a Covenant with a family.

The First Murder

Read Genesis 4:1-16, the story of Cain and Abel.

From the scripture passages fill in the following blanks:-

From Genesis 4:2

Abel becomes _______________________________

Cain becomes _______________________________________

In 4:4 Cain brings to the Lord _______________________

In 4:5 Abel brings to the Lord _______________________

The offerings that the two brothers bring and their relationship with God are very important. During this course we will be looking at the various offerings and their consequences. The important point to ponder at this stage is the state of the heart.

How does Cain respond to God in Genesis 4:5?

____

God gives Cain an opportunity to resist the sin that he is falling towards.

The word of God is spoken into his life in Genesis 4:7. Write it down.

____

____

____

Cain can master sin if he walks in obedience to God's Word. The power of sin is destroyed by the power of God's Word but we have to agree with it. Sadly Cain does not agree with the Word of God and subsequently he kills his brother. The blood of Abel cries out for justice and God hears that cry by banishing Cain from His presence. Cain needs protection so God 'puts a mark on Cain lest anyone kill him on sight'. The world has become a dangerous place in a very short time since the fall into sin.

The mark that God puts on Cain is the covenant mark, the visible seal or testimony of the covenant. Anybody seeing Cain with a mark on his forehead will know he is in covenant (the ancients understood covenant far better than modern man) and let him live peacefully. Consequently Cain can marry and have offspring which is in the rest of Genesis 4.

The first murder was caused because of one man's relationship with God. God is the excuse not the reason. The reason for the murder is the depravity in Cain's heart and his unwillingness to hear God's Word which is trying to turn him from sin.

The sons of God and daughters of men

Read Genesis 6:2. It separates humanity into two types of people, the sons of God and the daughters of men.[44] In Hebrew it reads more precisely 'the sons of Elohim and the daughters of Adam'.

'Elohim'

Hebrew for 'God'

'Adam'

Hebrew for 'man'

Genesis 4 details the generations of the sons of men. These are the descendants of Cain. Genesis 5 details the generations of the sons of God. These are the descendants of Seth. The two lines are separated by the action of Cain in Genesis 4:16 and Seth in Genesis 4:26.[45]

What does Genesis 4:16 say Cain did? ____

What happens in Genesis 4:26 in respect of God's name?

____

There is a common biblical theme associated with the invocation of God's name. The person who invokes God's name makes Him present. The New Jerusalem bible translates Genesis 4:26 as follows; 'Enosh was the first to invoke God's name'. He is Seth's firstborn son. Thus throughout Seth's family line with his generations calling on God's name, God becomes present to them and they are holy. They are so holy that something quite unique happens to Enoch.

What happens to Enoch in Genesis 5:24?

____

Cain's line is very worldly; his son Enoch has a city named after him demonstrating the worldly culture that exists.[46] Seth's line is holy to the extent that his descendant, Enoch, walks with God. He is taken straight to heaven.

Read Hebrews 11:5. What did Enoch do in respect to his relationship with God before he was taken up?

____

Contrast this with the line of Cain. The sixth person in his line is Lamech who marries two women (Polygamy) and commits murder against a young man.

What is his response to the murder in Genesis 4:24?

____

Lamech is the sixth generation from Cain. Six is man's number and represents imperfection.

The similarities between the two family lines are very striking. The names have similar characteristics but one major difference. One invokes the name of God; the other has left the presence of God. To invoke God's name is to dwell in his presence because God makes himself present when his name is invoked!

The Flood

The holy line of Seth is keeping the world in one piece and stops God's hand from striking, but when the two lines mix in Genesis 6:2 with the sons of God (Seth's line) intermarrying with the daughters of men (Cain's line), morality declines and God has to chastise sinful humanity.

Genesis 6:4 has the declaration about the nephilim. The word nephilim is from the Hebrew:-

Naphal – fallen

Nephilim – fallen ones

In Genesis 6:3 what does God say cannot remain because of sin (since he is but flesh)?

____

Also in Genesis 6:3 how long does humanity have before the flood comes?

____

Noah is found to be unique amongst humanity and his relationship with God is shown in Genesis 6:8. What sets him apart?

____

The world may not seem a bad place to us, but God sees differently. How does God see the world of that time in Genesis 6:11 that caused him to exercise judgement?

____

In Genesis 6:13-22 God reveals his plan to Noah. The prophet Amos tell us 'The Lord does nothing without revealing his plan to his servants, the prophets' (Amos 3:7).

How does Noah respond to the Word of God in Genesis 6:22?

____

Read Hebrews 11:7. What does Noah inherit as a result of his obedience?

____

According to Genesis 1:9 the water was gathered into its basin and the land was in one place. The post flood world is obviously very different with the land in many places and the waters also in many 'basins'. Was it just rain that caused this?

Where does the water come from in Genesis 7:11?

____

The Hebrew word for 'Abyss', 'great deep' is the same as in Genesis 1:2 'darkness was upon the face of *the deep*'.
According to Genesis 7:2 how many 'clean' animals were taken in the ark?

____

And how many unclean?

____

The bible is very clear about when the flood started (Genesis 7:11) and how long it rained for.
How deep were the waters according to Genesis 7:20?

____

How long did the flood last according to Genesis 7:24?

____

In Genesis 8:7 Noah releases a bird. What is the bird and what does it do?

____

The raven symbolises sin. The flying back and forth is a parallel with the Spirit of God in *Genesis 1:2* which was hovering upon the waters. Sadly sin is now the dominant force.
Noah also sends out another bird in Genesis 8:8-12. What is the bird, how many times is it sent out and what does the bird bring back?

____

____

The dove is a sign of the Holy Spirit.[47] The olive branch is a sign of the anointing.
God blesses Noah and his sons in a similar fashion to Adam and Eve in Genesis 9:1 and 7. *What is the blessing?*

____

How many times does God use the word 'covenant' in chapter 9?

____

What is the sign of the covenant, the visible testimony, and the promise of God associated with the sign of the covenant?
This is found in Genesis 9:12-15

____

The covenant with Noah remains in force during the times of the Gentiles, until the universal proclamation of the Gospel. The Bible venerates several great figures among the Gentiles: Abel the just, the king-priest Melchizedek – a figure of Christ – and the upright 'Noah, Daniel, and Job. Scripture thus expresses the heights of sanctity that can be reached by those who live according to the covenant of Noah, waiting for Christ to 'gather into one the children of God who are scattered abroad'. CCC 58

40!

- The rain lasted for 40 days and nights

- Forty signifies the span of time necessary for the ripening process that leads to fruition. For example, the gestation of an embryo from conception to birth.[48]
- Moses spent 40 days and nights in God's presence on Mount Sinai (Dt. 10:10)
- Israel spent 40 years in the wilderness for being disobedient and rebellious following the exodus from Egypt (Nm. 14:34)
- Elijah spent 40 days and nights walking to Horeb (1 Kings19:8)
- Ezekiel spent 40 days lying on his side in repentance for the sins of Israel (Ez. 4:6)
- The people of Nineveh were given 40 days to repent (Jonah 3:4)
- 40 days Jesus spent in the desert being tempted

After the flood the ages of the patriarchs change dramatically.
For example before the flood in Genesis 5:27 how long did Methuselah live?

____

Genesis 9:29, how long does Noah live for? (Noah is the last of the pre-flood patriarchs).

____

In Genesis 11 the Word of God follows Shem's descendants. How long did Shem live for according to Genesis 11:10 and 11?

____

Contrast that with Nahor who is the seventh descendant from Shem.
How long does he live according to Genesis 11:24 and 25?

____

After Nahor the average life span is dramatically reduced from the pre-flood world. In many commentaries this is largely explained away as being due to inaccurate records or imaginative chroniclers. Scientists also tend to ridicule the idea of people living for 500 years or more. However, it is not unreasonable to accept the life spans of the patriarchs as factual. Modern scientists know next to nothing about the aging process and therefore have no grounds whatsoever for criticizing the biblical account. St Augustine refuted those who tried to whittle down the ages of the patriarchs to agree with contemporary lifetimes.[49]

Seth to Abram and Melchizedech
In Genesis 5 count the descendants from Adam to Noah.
How many are there? _______________

These are the pre-flood patriarchs who lived for extraordinary long periods. In fact this is the way we were meant to live before sin had its devastating effect. If not for sin Adam would still be alive, as would all his descendants up to and including you.

Now count the post flood patriarchs up to and including Abram.
Genesis 11:10 to 11:26________

There are ten generations from Adam to the flood and ten generations from the flood to Abram. The pre flood patriarchal line ends with Noah. The post flood patriarchal line begins with Shem and ends with Abram who is also the first of the Hebrew patriarchs.

Shem (Hebrew)

Means 'name'

Fame, renown, reputation, character

When Abram is born Seth is 450 and still has 150 years left to live. In fact, Noah died only two years before Abram was born which sheds a different light on matters, especially considering that biblical history, as well as being inspired, was passed down from one generation to the next.[50]

Read Genesis 14:18-20. How is Melchizedek described?

____

This is the role that Adam held, and that he would have passed to an appropriate descendant. The title 'Priest of God Most High' (El Elyon) and 'High Priest in the order of Melchizedek.'

Melchizedek

Hebrew for

My King of Righteousness

Malki = My King

Tzedek = Righteousness

Melchizedek is called 'king of salem' which translates as

Melek Shalem

King of peace

The name Salem was an early name for Jerusalem.[51] Thus this person is the king of righteousness, king of peace and the priest of God Most High.

Referring back to Adam's line, what title or 'name' is given to the last of the ten pre flood patriarchs, Noah, in Genesis 6:9, 10? What does it say about him?

____

Depending on the translation it should tell us that Noah was a righteous man. Thus Noah is the last pre-flood 'king of righteousness'. He has to pass a blessing onto his first born son, a blessing that would enable him to walk in his relationship with God because Noah 'walked with God.'

To be righteous means to be in 'right-standing' with somebody. If we have righteousness with God it means we can approach God and he will listen to us. He will talk to us. God wants us to have this gift because it enables us to have relationship with one another. Thus for the early patriarchs to pass the gift on from one to another was of great importance.

Noah passes on the gift of righteousness to his firstborn son, Shem, who becomes the 'king of righteousness (Melchizedek) and king of Salem (peace).'[52]

Genesis 14:20. What does Abram give to Melchizedek?

____

In the bible it is always the lesser person who tithes to the greater person. Thus we are supposed to give our tithe to God. When Abram, the man who has relationship with God Most High and becomes the mediator of the covenant, tithes to Melchizedek it means that Melchizedek is greater than Abram.

Melchizedek blesses Abram. The greater blesses the lesser, the 'father' blesses the 'son.'

Read Genesis 15:6. Write it below.

____

Thus Abram who is blessed by Shem, the first of the post flood patriarchs, is blessed by God who 'credits' him with righteousness because of Abram's act of faith.

Read Hebrews 7:1-17. What does verse 3 say about Melchizedek?

____

Because Shem is the first of the post flood patriarchs he is regarded as having no ancestry.[53] The next person in line is the last of the pre flood patriarchs. Shem is the first in the line.

Abram receives the grace of righteousness and passes it to his sons. When the law is given men seek to be righteous by law, but when Jesus comes, dies, and rises we receive a great grace.

Write out 2 Corinthian 5:21

____

What does Matthew 6:33 say about what we should seek above all other things?

____

Daily meditations and readings:

Meditations Readings

Day one: Hebrews 11:7 Genesis 6

Day two: 2 Peter 2:5 Genesis 7

Day three: Sirach 44:17 Genesis 8

Day four: Psalm 110:4 Genesis 9

Day five: Hebrews 7 Hebrews 6:20

Day six: Genesis 15 Acts 3:13

Day seven: Genesis 17 John 8:58

5, Abraham, a covenant with a tribe

Abraham is considered to be the Father of the Jews, Christians and Muslims. Even if we all approach God in different ways he connects us. Consequently his life is very important.

The Catechism calls him a 'model of obedience' for all who have faith.[54]

When Abraham begins his walk with God he is called Abram which means 'Exalted Father'. We shall examine the name change as part of this study.

Read Genesis 12:1-4. Write down all the statements quoting the action of God (ie. 'I will bless you').

____

____

____

When you read 'God said' or 'The LORD said' in the Old Testament, substitute 'Jesus' so that you can see that the God of the Old is the same as the God of the new, who is the same as your God today. God does not change, mankind does.

LORD in capital letters

Means in Hebrew – YHWH

God, Father, Son and Holy Spirit

Thus, the Father calls Abram

Through the Son

In the power of the Holy Spirit

Read Genesis 12:4. How old is Abram when God calls him?

____

Like the Apostles after him Abram leaves his homeland for a strange land following God's call. Unlike the apostles Abram does not have the benefit of several thousand years of examples of faith to look to. However, he does have the unwritten oral tradition passed down from Adam, through to Noah, Shem, and down to him. Thus he knows there is a God who is sovereign and Almighty.

God's covenant with Abram takes several stages which are also a clear sign of God deepening his relationship with Abram. God leads Abram out of a life of possible idolatry in Haran. However, although we can view these stages of growth as a clear sign of God's hand on Abram's life it is worth bearing in mind that the call was over many years and Abram suffered many trials in the process. Daily life may have been very different to the picture presented in the scriptures which give us the key points in God's relationship with Abram. An overview of the story may yield the following:-

- Genesis 12 – God calls Abram, revealing Himself and the promise of a land in which Abram and his descendants will live.
- Genesis 15 – God further reveals Himself and cuts covenant
- Genesis 17 – Covenant of circumcision established, promise of a child is established in 'time'
- Genesis 18 – God leads Abraham into intercession demonstrating the power of the covenant.
- Genesis 21 – The child, Isaac, the promise of God, is born to Sarah.
- Genesis 22 – Abraham is tested by being asked to sacrifice his son.

What does God say to Abram in Genesis 15:1?

____

Calling to mind the various aspects of a covenant, God is giving Abram Himself as a shield of protection. He is also promising that Abram's reward will be very great, thus the promise of riches from a place of poverty.

Read Genesis 15:6. What does Abram do and how does God respond?

____

____

The gift of righteousness is absolutely vital for an ongoing relationship with God. By crediting Abram with this gift it enables Abram to approach God in prayer and petition him without fear. Righteousness can be called 'right standing,' meaning God has put Abram on an 'equal standing' with him.

Saint Paul spent a substantial part of his writing on this topic and it caused a lot of problems at the time of the reformation.

Read Romans 4:1-8. Write out verses 7 and 8.

____

____

God has given you a similar grace. Read 2 Corinthians 5:21. What does it say about righteousness?

____

God promises Abram the land of Canaan and Abram asks a very similar question to Mary in *Luke 1. "How am I to know I shall possess it?'* God then cuts covenant with Abram in much the same way as described in the 9 steps of a Hebrew Covenant ritual.

Genesis 15:9, 10 what does Abram do with the animals?

____

The birds of prey are a foreshadowing of the temptations that Satan put Jesus through in Luke 4. Abram stays with the sacrifice irrespective of the birds that are trying to destroy the covenant.[55]

What happens to Abram in Genesis 15:12?

____

The Hebrew word for 'trance', or 'sleep' is the same as used of Adam in Genesis 2:21 when God was creating woman.

Tardemah (Hebrew)

A deep sleep, Ecstacy

- Adam slept when God brought forth woman.
- Abraham slept when God established covenant
- Jesus 'slept' the death of the cross when he established covenant and brought forth from his side the bride of Christ.[56]

While Abram is in the deep sleep God tells him what will happen to his descendants and how he will rescue them from the hands of the Egyptians.

According to God in Genesis 15:16 what is the reason for Israel wiping out the Amorites that currently hold power in the Promised Land?

____

While Abram is in the trance what passes between the pieces of animal in Genesis 15:17?

____

These represent the pre-incarnate Christ and the Holy Spirit.[57] They are the two advocates of the covenant, the two mediators. One of the mediators has to pay the price for a broken covenant. Abram cannot do this so he cannot cut covenant. Jesus will ultimately pay the price but he will go back to his Father. So yet another advocate will be required.

Read John 14:16. Who is the other advocate?

____

Jesus is cutting covenant on behalf of Abram/humanity. The Holy Spirit is cutting covenant on behalf of God. God gives Abram the promise of the land of Canaan. This is the covenant promise and is a foreshadowing of the kingdom of God.

The Covenant of Circumcision

Read Genesis 17:1-22. 24 years after Abram is first called God establishes the covenant of circumcision.

At this point God reveals himself to Abram as 'God Almighty' or 'El Shaddai'. This name is very important to both the Jews and to Catholics.

El Shaddai (Hebrew)

'God Almighty'

'I believe in God, the Father, the Almighty'.

Each name of God is very important and shows a different side of his nature. The name 'El Shaddai' reveals God's mighty power. God displays his power at its height by freely forgiving sins.[58] When God reveals this name to Abram he makes a declaration.

Read Genesis 17:1. After God reveals himself as God Almighty what does he request of Abram?

____

Thus Abram is no longer able to live as he wants. He has made mistakes in his walk to this point but God is calling him deeper. God now wants Abram to walk in his presence (Consider Cain who was exiled from God's presence) and to be blameless: to stop sinning.[59] Under normal circumstances this would be a difficult call, but because God has spoken his creative work it enables Abram to do what God is calling him to do.

Read Genesis 17:4, 5. What is Abram's name changed to and what is his new mission in life?

____

____

God's covenant is to take Abram from being fatherless to being a father of a host of nations. His name change reflects this and brings with it a new nature and a new mission in life.

Abraham

Father of a multitude.

Abram takes the 'ah' from 'Yahweh'; God takes the name 'Abraham.' Thus Abraham has God's name inserted in his and belongs to God. God has Abraham's name and becomes 'the God of Abraham'; a Covenant exchange.[60]

Consider that all the time Abram has been called 'exalted father' he has been childless. To have been childless would have been a cause of great shame in that part of the world in that era, to have also been called 'exalted father' would have been a great humiliation. Perhaps this is one reason Abraham was so open to the presence and power of God.

Read Genesis 17:9-12. How is the covenant defined in verse 11?

____

From now on every male descendant of Abraham must be circumcised. The flesh of their foreskin must be cut off as a sign of the covenant. Under normal circumstances the sign of the covenant should be visible to ward off the enemy, however, Abraham serves an invisible God so the sign must be invisible. He must live by faith not by sight.

Some ask 'Why did God want the male genitals circumcised'? The genitals are the source of life, where the seed of life comes from the father to continue the human race. It is a sign that the seed of life, the Word of God, comes from

God the Father to lead the human race to eternal life. The stripping of the foreskin is a sign of the stripping of our outer self, our sin, so that we can walk in holiness.

Genesis 22, the testing of Abraham.

How does Genesis 22:2 describe Isaac in respect to Abraham?

____

How does John 3:16 describe Jesus in relation to the Father?

____

Mount Moriah is a mountain range upon which Jerusalem is built and where Calvary is located. Thus the sacrifice of Abraham, (the exalted Father), and Isaac, (his only son), is foreshadowing that of God, (The Exalted Father), and Jesus Christ, (His only begotten Son).

Read Genesis 22:4. On which day does Abraham see the place of sacrifice?

____

This foreshadows the day on which Jesus rose from the dead.

Genesis 22:6. What does Abraham lay on the shoulder of Isaac, and what does Abraham carry?

____

____

This reflects the Father who holds the fire of love and is the source of the Word of God *(John 7:16 'My teaching is not my own but comes from the one who sent me')*

Knife

Hebrew – Maakeleth

'To eat'

The knife represents the Word of God

We are invited to eat God's Word.

To feast on the flesh of the Son of God.

Abraham continues on his pilgrimage of faith:-

"When they came to the place of which God had told him, Abraham built an altar there and arranged the wood on it. Next he tied up his son Isaac, and put him on top of the wood on the altar. Then he reached out and took the knife to slaughter his son. But the LORD'S messenger called to him from heaven, "Abraham, Abraham!" "Yes, Lord," he answered. "Do not lay your hand on the boy," said the messenger. "Do not do the least thing to him. I know now how devoted you are to God, since you did not withhold from me your own beloved son."

Summing up

- God took the initiative and cut covenant with Abraham
- Satan tried to the consume sacrifice before covenant could be cut, ie vultures, the temptations of Jesus.
- God put Abraham to sleep to keep him from interfering. It is all done by God through the power of divine grace.
- The pre-incarnate Christ takes Abraham's place in the ceremony. Christ is Abraham's substitute
- Abram becomes a friend of God and takes God's name
- God becomes a friend of Abraham and takes Abraham's name.
- Abraham believes in the promise and is declared righteous by God
- God fulfils His promise regarding Abraham's seed

What did Abraham believe?

- He believed in a supernatural birth, that God would supernaturally bring a son into the world.
- He believed enough that for three days his son was dead because the journey was begun on the first day and it is on the 'third day' they see the place of sacrifice. For the duration of that journey Abraham believed Isaac was as good as dead.
- Abraham believed that God would provide a substitute sacrifice, or would raise Isaac from the dead – resurrection.
- Abraham believed that on that mountain God would provide a substitute sacrifice and it would be seen on that very mountain.[61]

All of this is a foreshadowing of what Jesus the Messiah does for us. God is speaking to us through his people in the Old Testament in order to prepare them for when Jesus arrives. Although the language is veiled it is only so until it is viewed in the light of the New Testament, the covenant established in the blood of Jesus. If we view the Old Testament in the light of the cross it makes sense.

Read Hebrews 11:17-19. What does it say about Abraham's willingness to sacrifice his son?

____

____

At the point that Abraham is going to kill his son at God's command God reveals himself to Abraham as:-

YHWH Yirreh

'God provides'

Or more accurately

'God sees'

When we look at the phrase 'God provides' the first occurrence is at the Abrahamic sacrifice of Isaac, where God provides a 'ram'. Thus the provision of God is first and foremost in respect of our salvation. God is not providing any material goods for Abraham. In fact Abraham has received many material goods up to this point and was considered a wealthy man. It is at this point that God is showing Abraham a small vision of his plan of salvation, 'I myself will provide a ram'.

It is also on this mountain that the modern name for Jerusalem is given. In ancient times Jerusalem was known as 'salem.'[62] If we take the Hebrew word for 'provides' and add it to salem we have 'Yirreh-salem', or 'Jeru-salem'[63] (note that the letter 'J' does not occur in Hebrew). If we apply this to the story of Abraham and Isaac we could say that God will 'provide peace,' or will 'see peace' on this mountain. It will be at the crucifixion that God will finally see peace on earth when Jesus establishes communion between God and man.

This salvation is fulfilled in Christ who tells us in Matthew 6 not to worry about what we are to eat or drink but to:- 'Seek first the kingdom of God and its righteousness and all these other things will be added to you' (Mt. 6:33).

Daily meditations and readings:-

Meditations Readings

Day one: Genesis 15:1 Psalm 23

Day two: Genesis 17:1 Hebrews 11

Day three: Genesis 22:14 Matthew 6

Day four: Hebrews 11:17 John 3

Day five: Hebrews 10:16 Ezekiel 36
Day six: Hebrews 7:22 Psalm 89
Day seven: Hebrews 11:23 Exodus 2

6. Moses – a covenant with a nation.

The introduction to this chapter is found in the book of Exodus. Read chapter1 in its entirety and then chapter two up to verse 10.

The people of Israel are held in captivity as God told Abraham they would be. However, as God also said, their time in captivity is coming to an end. They were given 450 years. Consequently God is preparing to raise up a man who will lead them out of their captivity. Moses is that man.

Write out Exodus 2:10

____

Moses

Hebrew = Moshe

'I drew him out'

Moses was raised in the Egyptian royal family and was considered to be the firstborn son of Pharaoh's daughter, and a potential heir to the throne. His Egyptian name reflects this. Egyptian Pharaoh's were named after their gods because they believed, like the Roman Caesar's after them, that their leaders were divine. Hence:-

Ra-meses Drawn out of the sun god 'ra'

Tut-moses Drawn out of the god 'tut'

Hapi-Moshe Drawn out of the nile god 'hapi'

Once Moses gets in touch with his Hebrew roots he changes his name to Moshe, dropping the name of the false god 'Hapi'.

Moses:-

- spends 40 years being raised in the Pharaoh's court,
- 40 years in the desert herding sheep and raising a family.
- 40 years leading Israel towards the Promised Land

The Revelation of God

The oppression of Israel increases while Moses is in exile in the desert near Sinai. It gets to the point that the people cry out to God.

Read Exodus 2:23-25. What is God's response to Israel's cry for release?

____

____

It is because of his covenant with the forefathers of the Hebrews that God hears the cry of his people and 'comes down' to rescue them. The scriptures talk several times about God 'coming down'. The first time was at Babel in judgement. Another time was at the incarnation. The last time God comes down will be at the second coming of Christ.

Read Exodus 3:2. What surprises Moses?

____

In his time in the desert it was common for him to see burning bushes. The Rabbis say that the bush was of the Acacia variety. These bushes have oil in the stem and are prone to burst into flames in the hot desert climate. Consequently Moses may well have seen many burning bushes. The difference in this circumstance is that the bush is not consumed.

Moses has to ask God's name because the Egypt he left behind had many gods with many different names and many different purposes.

Read Exodus 3:14 and 15. What is God's name?

____

____

God has to reveal his name, and thus his character for several reasons.

- Egypt has many gods with many names. Moses knew them all. Which one was this?
- If Moses is to go in the name of God, what name can he use? I.e, 'open up in the name of the king'. The power is in the name!
- God's revealed name 'I am', also known as 'Yahweh,' is the name by which God redeemed Israel from Egypt.
- To disclose one's name is to make oneself known to others; in a way it is to hand oneself over by become accessible, capable of being known more intimately and addressed personally.[64]
- The revelation that proved to be the fundamental one for both the Old and New Covenants was the revelation of the divine name to Moses in the theophany of the burning bush.[65]

Read Exodus 3:1 – 4:17, the call of Moses. There are several aspects to the encounter:

- The revelation of God's name (Ex. 3:6-15).
- The mission of Moses (Ex. 3:10- 4:17)
- Moses reluctance and inadequacy (Ex. 4:1-14) (As with Isaiah and Jeremiah!)
- God's response with signs and wonders (Ex. 4:2-7).
- God permits Moses to have Aaron as his mouthpiece (Ex. 4:14).
- Exodus 4:15, the commission.

Write out Exodus 4:15.

____

____

Read John 7:16.

God is the one who gives us words to speak and actions to do. Jesus was one who only spoke what his Father taught him and only did as his Father was doing.

Exodus 7:14 – 11:10. The ten plagues; each plague is a judgement on a different demon god of Egypt:–

1. Water turned into blood (Hapi – the god of the Nile)
2. Frogs (Hecate)

1. Gnats would have used the dead frogs for breeding grounds symbolizing the scarab beetle (Geb) – magicians acknowledge the 'finger' of God.
2. Flies would have also used the dead frogs for breeding grounds (Beelzebul)
3. Pestilence. (the Bull god, Apis)
4. Boils (Imhotep – a deified layman)
5. Hail (destroyed trees and plants which were used in pagan worship)

6. Locusts (Serapis who was supposed to protect against locusts)
7. Darkness (Ra)
8. First born (Molech)

By using natural phenomena to bring about the liberation of his people, God demonstrated to Israelites and Egyptians alike that he was the Lord of nature. In addition, each plague was directed against the Egyptian religion.[66]

Read Exodus 8:11 or 8:15 (depending on your bible translation). What is Pharaoh's response?

____

____

For the first five plagues Pharaoh hardens his heart. For the last five plagues there is a different scenario.
What does God do to Pharaoh in Exodus 9:12?

____

Pharaoh made his own heart hard; then God made Pharaoh's heart hard. In other words God hands him over to his own hard heart. This is one of the ways God approaches mankind's insistence on remaining in sin. Read Romans 1:18 which talks about the wrath of God.
Write out Romans 1:24, 26, and 28 which shows God handing over mankind to sin.

____

____

____

To understand this further please read Romans 9:16-23 and Romans 11:30-36.
The Passover
There are many parallels in this story with that of the passion of Jesus. Also, where the book of Exodus refers to 'God' or 'LORD' it is referring to the Father, Son and Holy Spirit. Thus the Passover instructions are being given by Jesus. Also note that Jesus is giving instructions for a feast in Israel (Passover) that foreshadows his own passion over a thousand years later. The language is veiled because the mystery must be understood by faith. Nobody can enter into God's kingdom except by faith.

Read Exodus 11 where God warns about the death of the firstborn.
Read Exodus 12 where God give details for the Passover.
In Exodus 12:13 what is going to protect the firstborn of Israel from death?

____

What happens in Exodus 12:3?

____

How long is the Passover lamb kept in the house before it is slaughtered in verse 6?

____

The blood of the lamb is the power of the covenant. Those who accept the blood covering leave Egypt (which symbolises sin) with their lives. Those who reject the blood die in Egypt (in their sin). It is the blood which redeems (cf. 1 Pet. 1:18, 19).

In Exodus 12:12 who is God executing judgment on?

____

Write out Exodus 12:22.

____

The horizontal beam (lintel) and the two vertical beams foreshadow the cross of Jesus. The blood and water (from the hyssop stick) foreshadow the blood and water from the side of Christ.

In Exodus 12:23, who kills the firstborn?

The Destroyer cannot attack the Israelites who have sprinkled their doorposts and lintel with blood because of the power of God's Word which protects. God said 'Seeing the blood I will pass over you and no destructive blow will come upon you'. (Exodus 12:13*)*. This is the word that protects Israel. They cooperate with God's plan by doing as his word tells them.

In Exodus 13:2 what does God want to happen with the firstborn of Israel?

Compare this with the firstborn of the Egyptians who were killed due to the sin of Egypt.

Why the firstborn?

Every firstborn child is the one who 'opens the womb'. Thus it is the firstborn child who is a 'virgin birth' – it is the first birth that the mother has had. This is a foreshadowing of the birth of Christ who is the virgin birth in every respect.

Read Exodus 14. The people pass through the Red sea – by faith.

Write out Exodus 15:1

The Hebrew word for 'sing' should translate as 'will sing'. Ie, it is future tense. Thus the scriptures are saying that Moses will sing when Israel pass through the waters. Given that the waters of the Red Sea are a foreshadowing of baptism when we accept Jesus as Lord and Saviour, the Word of God is declaring that Moses will sing to the Lord when Israel receives baptism and accepts Jesus as Lord and Saviour.

The Waters of Marah

Read Exodus 15:22-27. Why couldn't the Israelites drink the water?

The waters in this area of the desert have a high concentration of Magnesium and Calcium. The Magnesium acts as a powerful laxative which gives the drinker severe stomach cramps. The Calcium is a powerful energy supplement for athletes.

The Magnesium would have cleansed their bodies of the non-kosher food they constantly ate in Egypt. The cramping effect would have cleansed their souls. Although the Israelites were no longer in Egypt, Egypt was still very much in them.[67]

The Calcium was meant to help them get through the desert in record time. It should have taken them about 11 days according to some commentators. Unfortunately it took 40 years!

In Exodus 15:25 how does Moses make the bitter waters sweet?

The trees are still beside the waters to this day. The sap from the branches causes the bitter minerals in the waters to sink to the bottom making the water sweet.[68]

The tree, which translates from Hebrew as 'wood' is a foreshadowing of the wood of the cross. This is the wood that gives meaning to our suffering and self denial. Everything we suffer and endure with joy in this life adds to our eternal reward thanks to the power of the cross.

Write out Exodus 15:26

God speaks of healing when Israel are at the bitter waters (bitter = Marah). This is where God reveals himself as 'Yahweh Rofe', God who heals. Note, the revelation of God as healer takes place at the bitter waters, not at the waters of Elim which are fresh. The bitter waters were good for Israel as they are good for us. Are you in a 'bitter place' in your life? Only the wood of the cross can make it sweet.

Exodus 19, Israel at Mount Sinai. Ch. 20, the Ten Commandments. (covenant terms)
Summarise each of the commandments.

1. ____

1. ____

1. ____

1. ____

1. ____

1. ____

1. ____

1. ____

1. ____

1. ____

Whereas the ten plagues had come on the Egyptians who worshipped demons and refused to repent, the Ten Commandments are given to the Jews who worship God.

The first three commandments are regarding God. The final six are regarding us. The connecting commandment is the Sabbath which serves to connect man to God.

The law is given. Sin has existed, but there is no law to enforce it. Now the law is given and what was previously acceptable is now illegal (ie, no speed limit means I can drive as fast as I like, but a speed limit sign is now put up and enforced!). Sadly, even though there is a speed limit sign I do not want to obey it. This is the problem with the law. However, when Jesus comes he brings the law of grace which enables me to live according to the law of God, the law of love. God gives the law as a 'pedagogue' to lead his people towards Christ and enkindle a desire for the Holy Spirit.[69]

Read Exodus 24: the covenant with the nation of Israel.
What does Moses do with the book of the covenant?

____

What does Moses do with the blood?

____

What do the Israelites declare in Exodus 24:7?

____

What does Moses declare in Exodus 24:8?

____

Compare these words with those of Jesus Christ in Luke 22:20

____

Write out Exodus 32:15, 16:

____

____

____

The Rabbis think of this as the first Pentecost, when Moses brought the law down from Mount Sinai. They consider this to be the birthday of Judaism. Relate this to Acts 2 when Jesus sends the Holy Spirit down on the Apostles, the birthday of the Church. The Word and the Spirit come together, birthing first the Jews, then the Church.

A summary of Exodus 32:

- Whilst Moses is up the mountain with God the people get bored and make a golden calf
- The journey from Sinai to Canaan should take 11 days, but because of their complaining it took 40 years.
- Moses brings down the tablets and breaks them.
- Judgement came on the people because of their sin and 3000 died at the sword of the Levites because they refused to repent. Contrast this with Acts 2 when 3000 people live at the sword of the Spirit in the hands of the Apostles because they repent and receive the Holy Spirit.

Daily meditations and readings:-
(Where the Old Testament reads 'law' or 'statutes' read it as 'Word of God'.
Meditations Readings
Day one: Exodus 3:2 Exodus 3
Day two: Exodus 3:6 Deuteronomy 6
Day three: Exodus 6:2 Deuteronomy 30
Day four: Hebrews 4:9 Psalm 119
Day five: Hebrews 4:15 Psalm 51
Day six: Hebrews 10:14 Leviticus 23
Day seven: 1 Corinthian 1:18 Deuteronomy 4

7. The feasts, priesthood and the call to holiness.

Read Deuteronomy 6:1-6

What does God want us to be taught and observe in order that we may have a 'long life' (eternal life)?

____

____

What are the words in verse 6 that God wants to enjoin on us?

____

____

In Israel this scripture is known as the:-

'Shema'

Which means

'Hear'

It suggests a working out of what is spoken rather than an immediate understanding and application in daily life. We could say that the Shema is a seed being planted which takes time to mature; as opposed to a light being switched on which is immediate.

The Shema is very important to orthodox Jews. The Orthodox male will speak the Shema as soon as he wakes in the morning and before he falls asleep at night. It is said this is the first thing a young Jew will be taught and it is the last thing a Jew will speak before they die. Thus it is central to their faith.

When God led the people of Israel out of Egypt they were a people who had a God to worship but no liturgy through which to do this. For Christians it is a matter of course that when we go to church we adopt a certain mannerism, we carry out certain actions, speak certain words, we respond to our liturgy in an appropriate way. That was not the case with the Hebrews, so God had to teach them how to worship Him.

Deuteronomy 6 shows Jesus teaching Israel how to pray ('take these words to heart'), Matthew 6 shows Jesus teaching his disciples how to pray when he was on the mountain in Israel.

In Luke 11 the disciples approach Jesus and ask 'Lord, teach us how to pray'.
What does Jesus teach the disciples?

____

____

____

As with all things pertaining to God worship is done in an orderly way though it may not appear so at first sight.

- ***Exodus 25*** God establishes the temple for worship. The fittings for the temple, a priesthood to offer sacrifice with details for their special garments.
- ***Exodus 30-40*** the temple is built.
- ***Leviticus 1-7*** God establishes a system of sacrifice
- ***Leviticus 8*** the priests are ordained in order to offer the sacrifices within the temple.

God gives the Hebrews a set of laws so that they know how they should behave in the land God is giving them. If they fail to obey the laws God details the sacrifices through which they can make atonement. These laws are called:-

'Mitzvah'

Hebrew for

'Commandments'

God gives the Jews several feasts during the year as a pattern of life to live by. They also follow the harvest season so that the harvest begins and ends with pilgrimage and worship of God. These are called pilgrim feasts, in order to celebrate them correctly every man must leave his home, his work, his family, his place of security, and journey to what was considered to be the dwelling place of God to worship and offer sacrifice.

The 3 pilgrim feasts of Israel

What is the first feast in Leviticus 23:5?

____

The second feast in Leviticus 23:16 is on which day:

____

There are two other names for this feast. One is the feast of feast of first fruits. The other is in Numbers 28:26. What is it?

____

Leviticus 23:27 give us the third feast. What is it?

____

This final feast incorporates the following celebrations:-

- Rosh Hashanah - The head of the year/New year's day
- Yom Kippur – The day of atonement. Sacrifice is made for the sins of the world.
- Sukkot – Tabernacles. Everybody lives in a booth made of tree branches remembering their journey across the Sinai Wilderness.
- Illumination of the temple.
- Pouring of water. Water taken from pool of Siloam and mixed with wine at the foot of the sacrificial altar in the temple. Lasts for 7 days.
- Hoshanna Rabba – the day of the great hosanna.
- Simchat Torah – Rejoincing over the Torah. The Torah scroll is taken out of its place of safekeeping (a tabernacle) and is paraded around the synagogue in celebration.[70]

Deuteronomy 16:16

"Three times a year, then, every male among you shall appear before the Lord, your God, in the place which he chooses: at the feast of unleavened bread, at the feast of weeks, and at the feast of booths"

These are the three pilgrim feasts of Passover, Pentecost and Tabernacles. It can cause a bit of confusion because some believe that the feast of Pentecost is a predominantly Christian celebration. However, the Acts of the Apostles declares 'When the time for Pentecost was fulfilled....' (Acts 2:1). Thus the feast of Pentecost was already established. The very first Pentecost is shown in the book of Exodus.

Write out Exodus 32:15:-

____

____

This is the first Pentecost. It is the day on which Moses brings the stone tablets with the Ten Commandments written on them down from God's holy mountain. This is the birthday of Judaism. The Pentecost celebrated in Acts 2 is the day on which Jesus sends the Holy Spirit down on the Apostles, the early church. This is the birthday of the Church. The birthday of Judaism is the coming of God's Word. The birthday of the Church is the coming of the Spirit. Both celebrated on the same day.

If God's law was written on tablets of stone 'by the finger of God', then the 'letter from Christ' entrusted to the care of the apostles is written 'with the Spirit of the living God, not on tablets of stone, but on tablets of human hearts'.[71]

The Priesthood

In Exodus 19 the people gather at the foot of Mount Sinai in preparation for receiving God's Commandments, the code for them to live by. God speaks the following words among others.

Read Exodus 19:5, 6. What three promises does God make to the people of Israel in respect of their relationship with Him?

____

____

____

At this stage these promises are for the entire nation. However, sin isn't far away and while Moses is up the mountain the people give themselves over to idolatry and fornication.

Read Exodus 32 which gives us the behaviour of God's people while their leader is on the mountain with God. Which tribe rallies around Moses to carry out his command?

____

How many Israelites lose their lives at the sword of the Levites?

____

In Acts 2 how many men give their lives to Jesus at the sword of the Spirit in the hands of the Apostles?

____

In Exodus 32:29 what blessing did the Levites bring on themselves as a consequence of their action?

____

In Exodus 32:33 what is the punishment for idolatry, the making and worshipping of the golden calf?

____

When we look at this event from the perspective of modern mankind we may think God's action is quite harsh. However, there is a valuable lesson to be learnt. The initial punishment on the Israelites was death at the sword of the Levites. This is the same punishment for breaking several of the commandments. For example working on the Sabbath carries the death penalty. It is not so much a case of God systematically killing his people for failing to keep his laws, it is more a case of God showing us the consequence for sin and it goes back to Eden. 'If you eat of the tree of the knowledge of good and evil you will die'. The same consequence remains to this day. The penalty for sin is death. If we sin against God we suffer the temporal death of separating ourselves from God's life. If we die in a state of mortal sin without repenting we suffer the eternal consequence of eternal death, eternal separation from the life of God. This is not the punishment that God imposes on us; it is the choice we make. If we have chosen the path of sin, then we have rejected God and chosen self.[72]

Because the Israelites have sinned against God by entering in to idolatry they lose the blessing of priesthood. On the other hand the Levites, by carrying out God's command, enter into the blessing and receive the priesthood.

Read Exodus 28:1,2

Who is God telling Moses to bring into his presence as priests?

____

The High priesthood of Israel is given to Aaron and his sons. This means they carry out the sacrifices and are granted entrance into the holy of holies where the Ark of the Covenant is kept, they make atonement on behalf of the people of Israel and the world. Thus the priesthood has gone from a whole nation to just 5 men.

Leviticus chapters 8 and 9 detail the ordination of Aaron and his sons. In Leviticus 8:5 and 6 what is the first thing that Moses does to prepare Aaron and his sons for the priesthood?

____

This is a foreshadowing of baptism, when we are washed in water to become a 'royal priesthood' (cf. 1 Peter 2:9).

Moses follows up the baptism of water with an anointing in Leviticus 8:12. What is he anointed with and what is the effect of the anointing?

———

Leviticus 9:1. On which day does Moses summon Aaron and his sons?

———————————————

In Leviticus 9:4, 6, Aaron and his sons are given instructions to make certain sacrifices in order that God may do what?

———————————————————————————————

One of these sacrifices is called a 'peace offering' and is intended to make peace between God and man. The Hebrew word is 'Shelem' which means 'a sacrifice for alliance or friendship'.

Read Luke 24:36. This is after the resurrection of Jesus when he reveals himself to his disciples. What does he say to them?

————————————————————————————

In order for God to reveals himself to mankind, man has to do something. We are the ones who sinned, we disobeyed God's simple request, and we have separated ourselves from God. God is not the one who has done anything bad in this relationship; mankind is.

Mankind needs to make amends; this is detailed in the book of Leviticus and fulfilled in Christ. One of the sacrifices is called the 'peace' offering which is offered in fulfilment of a vow (also called a fulfilment sacrifice). Jesus is the peace offering. He is the one who brings peace between God and man so that we can share fellowship once again. Hence, when he appears to his apostles he declares 'Shalom', because he has made the 'shelem' offering.

The priesthood decreases

Read Leviticus 10:1-5.

What do the two sons of Aaron offer to God?

————————————————————————————

When they have made their offering what happens?

————————————————————————————

————————————————————————————

Compare this with Leviticus 9:22-24 where Aaron makes a sacrifice and fire comes from the Lord's presence and consumes the sacrifice.

When we come before the Lord with a clear conscience and obeying that which he has said to us, we are blessed. If we come before the Lord in a state of serious sin with no sense of repentance, there is no blessing.

We choose!

The sacrifice that the sons of Aaron offered was called 'profane', or 'unauthorised' depending on the translation that is used. The original Hebrew word 'zur' can also mean 'strange'. The sons of Aaron had made an offering that was being done out of their own ego as newly ordained priests of God Most High. They had not been authorised to offer that sacrifice. One wonders if they were trying to recreate the fire that had occurred in Leviticus 9:24 when God manifested himself in the fire and consumed the sacrifice. If so it is a case of man putting God to the test and paying the penalty for such an act.

We should remember that we serve a holy God.

The Levites

Read Numbers 3:1-13

What role do the tribe of Levi have as a result of their action in the desert?

———

———

Aaron and his sons are consecrated to offer sacrifice, the wider tribe of Levi are consecrated, by their earlier actions, to serve the sons of Aaron. We could say that whereas the priesthood belongs to Aaron and his sons, the 'Diaconate' belongs to the Levites who assist the priests.

The call to holiness
As for the Israelites, all is not lost! Numbers 6 details the Nazirite vow. There are four aspects to it.
Numbers 6:2. What is the Israelite doing?

____

Numbers 6:3. What must the Nazirite abstain from?

____

Numbers 6:5. What must he do with his hair?

____

Numbers 6:6. What must he keep away from?

____

The Nazirite vow is for lay people who wish to be consecrated in a special way to God.

Summing up, there are three levels of consecration to God which can be compared to our Catholicism as follows:-
High priesthood through Aaron and his sons Priests
Levitical priesthood which serves the sons of Aaron Diaconate
Nazirite vow Consecrated lay people
All of this is to show how the people of God (Israel – Christians) are set apart in a special way to serve God. This is called holiness. Leviticus 19 details the calling to holiness which is further emphasised by the first Pope:-
Read 1 Peter 1:13-16
According to verse 15 what 'is' God?

____

As a consequence of what God 'is', what does God want us to 'be'?

____

The Call to Holiness
In 'Novo Millenio Inneunte' Pope John Paul II declares 'all pastoral initiatives should be set in relation to holiness'.[73] If a parish has a pastoral council the call to holiness should be top of the agenda. First Holy Communion classes should teach young children about the call to holiness. Confirmation classes should teach teenagers about the call to holiness. Everything a parish does should have holiness as the most important aspect of their walk with God.

For the Jewish community in the middle of the Sinai Wilderness the call to holiness was central to the law that God gave them.
Read Leviticus 19:1 and 2
There are two questions we need to ask ourselves in verse 1.
Who is God telling Moses to address?

____

What is he asking them to be?

____

The Hebrew word for holy is:-
'Kadosh'
Which means
'set apart'
To be holy simply means to be 'set apart' for God's purposes. The word 'consecrated' means the same thing. It means that we cannot behave as we want to, we must behave as God wants us to. Of course we do not have to obey what God is calling us to, but that thinking is simply rebellion and a person who disobeys God will ultimately be obeying Satan. We will always be walking in obedience to one way of thinking or another. It is nice to think that we are being our own

independent self, but that is not original. Satan did that many thousands of years ago and you would simply be following his ways.

The person who wants to walk in obedience to God's ways is the one who enters into eternal life. There may be a lot of failures whilst trying to walk in God's ways, but a person who is walking a path even if they keep falling down is still walking on that path.

The first thing that is called holy in the bible is the Sabbath.

Read Genesis 2:1-3. What does verse 3 say about the Sabbath?

____

In Jewish circles this is the most important day of the week, it is the perfect day.[74] It is the only day when they cannot do as they want to do; they have to obey God's ways on that day. God's ways tell them to do nothing. They have to rest. It is an extraordinary thing that even in 21st century western culture we are in so much rebellion against the reign of God that we even refuse to take a day of rest!

However, if God has blessed this day and it is the first thing he calls holy, then who are we to be disobedient.

In the Christian church the early Apostles changed the day of rest from the seventh day to the eighth (or first) day of the week. Saturday to Sunday. This was to honour the day of resurrection. The day when God creates all things new through the death and resurrection of His Son. This is the day we are invited to honour.

Holiness

Read Ephesians 1:1. Who does St Paul address the letter to?

____

Then read Philippians 1:1. Who is this addressed to?

____

Finally read Colossians 1:2. Who is addressed?

____

St Paul's letters emphasise this calling, several of them begin with the address 'to the holy ones' others with 'called to holiness'. Either way, the calling is there and means we are obliged, because of our faith, to examine our lives and respond to God's call. That means we can either reject it or accept it. However, to call ourselves Christians and then live as we see fit is not in line with being a Christian. To call ourselves Christians means living as Christ. Walking in His ways and practicing self-denial; loving our friends and our enemies. Walking in holiness; acknowledging our failings. Getting up when we fall into sin. Frequenting the sacraments; being fully alive.

Turning back to Leviticus 19 read verses 1 and 2 again.

In verse 2 who are we asked to respect/honour, and what are we asked to keep?

____

The first area of holiness is regarding our relationship with God. We are told to be holy because God is holy. If we want fellowship with God we have to be like him – holy.

The second area of holiness is our parents. For this we need to ask the question, when did our parents become our parents? This was when you were conceived as a result of their marital union. Thus we can say that the marriage act of sexual intercourse is meant to be holy. We make it unholy through the use of contraceptives and unnatural sexual practices. This also means that the second of area of holiness is in respect of our spouse.

The third area of holiness is the day of rest. If we want to walk in holiness we need to learn to obey God's call to rest and 'be' in his presence. Our eternity is going to be spent 'resting' in the presence of God. When we rest we spend time with God and our family.

Read 1 Corinthian 3:17. Who is the temple of God and what 'is' that temple?

____

It is true that we can still fall into sin. It is also true that we must not let sin have the final say. We can overcome sin through regular meditation on the Word of God and the power of divine grace. It is a slow and sometimes difficult journey but if we are committed to spend time in God's presence each and every day then God can use that time to cleanse us from sin and lead us in holiness. As always – we choose!

We are not alone in our struggle against sin and our walk in holiness.

Hebrews 12:1-7

"Therefore, since we are surrounded by so great a cloud of witnesses, let us rid ourselves of every burden and sin that clings to us and persevere in running the race that lies before us while keeping our eyes fixed on Jesus, the leader and perfecter of faith. For the sake of the joy that lay before him he endured the cross, despising its shame, and has taken his seat at the right of the throne of God. Consider how he endured such opposition from sinners, in order that you may not grow weary and lose heart. In your struggle against sin you have not yet resisted to the point of shedding blood. You have also forgotten the exhortation addressed to you as sons: "My son, do not disdain the discipline of the Lord or lose heart when reproved by him; for whom the Lord loves, he disciplines; he scourges every son he acknowledges." Endure your trials as "discipline"; God treats you as sons. For what "son" is there whom his father does not discipline?

From the Popes and Saints

There is only one choice; to live for self or to live for God.

Fr Gabriel of Saint Mary Magdalen

Nothing whatever pertaining to godliness and real holiness can be accomplished without grace.

Saint Augustine

All of us can attain to Christian virtue and holiness, no matter in what condition of life we live and no matter what our life work may be.

Saint Francis de Sales

All of us must be saints in this world. Holiness is a duty for you and me. So let's be saints and so give glory to the Father.

Mother Teresa

When I invite you to become saints, I am asking you not to be content with second best.

Pope Benedict XVI, Sports Arena of St Mary's University College, Twickenham, Friday, 17 September 2010

It is quite clear that all Christians in any state or walk of life are called to the fullness of Christian life and to the perfection of love, and by this holiness a more human life is fostered also in earthly society.

Lumen Gentium paragraph 40.

Daily meditations and readings
Meditations Readings
Day one: Hebrews 3:1 Hebrews 4
Day two: Leviticus 19:2 Leviticus 19
Day three: Genesis 2:3 Exodus 31:13-17
Day four: Leviticus 10:3 Ephesians 4
Day five: Hebrews 12:14 Hebrews 12
Day six: 1 Thess 3:13 Wisdom 6
Day seven: Wisdom 6:10 Ephesians 4

8. David – a covenant with a kingdom.

David anointed as king of Israel

When Israel entered into the Promised Land, for a period of time they were ruled by 'Judges' who were men and women God raised up to draw the people close to him. Time and time again the people of Israel would wander away from God; His response was to raise individuals who would draw them back; then they would wander away. Finally we come to the book of Samuel where God raises up the prophet Samuel, considered to be the last of the Judges.

Read 1 Samuel 8:1-7 and write out verse 7:-

____

Thus, because of the hardness of heart of the people who want to be like the nations around them, God permits them to have a king.

Read 1 Samuel 9:1-3 which introduces us to the person of Saul.
Then read 1 Samuel 10:1- 11. What will the Spirit of God do to Saul?

____

This tells us about the outpouring of the Holy Spirit, the breath of life. This gift enables Saul to fulfil his office provided he walks in holiness. Sadly Saul does not walk in holiness and sins against God.

Read 1 Samuel 13:4-14. Why did God reject Saul according to verses 13 and 14

____

(Where it says 'God's command' read 'God's Word')
Read 1 Samuel 15:11, 22-28. Once again, according to verse 23, why has Saul been rejected as king?

____

The passage above clearly shows that Saul has lost the anointing because of his sin, so God has to raise up another king who would seek Him rather than power. He finds that king tending sheep in Bethlehem.

Read 1 Samuel 16. What does God say to Samuel when David shows up?

____

What does Samuel do to David?

____

What does the Spirit of God do when Samuel has anointed David?

____

In verse 14 we read about King Saul. What or who has left him and what has been sent to torment him?

____

David, the anointed king of Israel in the Spirit of God, enters into the service of the king as his armor bearer and a court musician.

In 1 Samuel 16:23 what happens when David plays music for King Saul?

____

Thus, David is anointed as king and the Spirit of God is on him so powerfully that when he worships God Saul is set free from the evil spirit that plagues him. Sadly Saul is unrepentant and this leaves him open to be afflicted by that same evil spirit.

Anointed

Hebrew – Mashach

'To smear or rub with oil'

All kings and priests in Israel were anointed with oil

As a sign of the Holy Spirit who 'came upon' them

And enabled them to fulfil their office in life.

A time of warfare: David vs Goliath

1 Samuel 17 tells the story of the Philistines rallying against the Israelites. Goliath is the giant, rumoured to be the last of the Nephilim, who takes a stand against the people of God. The Philistines took their stand against Israel for a period of 40 days!

What is David's responce to the taunt of Goliath in 1 Sam 17:26.

____

As David declares his faith in God's ability to defeat Goliath those around him misunderstand his courage. They think David is going up to fight him in his own strength. His brothers and other soldiers are living according to the flesh. David is a man of faith who thinks in accordance with the Spirit.

Who does David say will help him and how in 1 Sam 17:37?

____

In 1 Sam 17:38, 39 Saul clothes David in his own warriors garments. David declares 'I cannot go in these because I have never tried them before' and he throws them off. This is a similar scenario to the previous comments; man's response to a dilemma in the natural that can only be solved in the power of God. David strips himself of man's words and man's ways and goes into the battle in God's way.

David's weapons are not of the flesh, they are of the Spirit. What are they according to 1 Samuel 17:40?

____

The five smooth stones symbolize the five books of the Torah that convert our stony hearts to the One, True Living God. In David's time these were probably the only writings available to the people of God, the five books of the Torah given to Moses on Mount Sinai. They are an apparently small weapon; but a mighty one.

1 Samuel 17:45 defines David's weapons. Not sword, not the five smooth stones. What?

____

It is the power that is in God's holy name that saves us from the evil one.

David's covenant with the house of Saul

Read 1 Samuel 18:1-5

Although David has been anointed king of Israel, he is not the rightful heir to the throne in the 'natural'. This is held by Jonathan, the first born son of King Saul. Thus, although David is King in the order of the Spirit, in the order of the flesh the kingdom will pass from Saul to Jonathan. However, God has everything in hand. Imagine being anointed for a specific purpose but somebody else is already fulfilling that purpose. The average person may get impatient, concerned, worried, wound up, angry, even bitter. However, God can bring all things to pass whilst we wait patiently.

Write verses 3 and 4 of 1 Samuel 18:-

____

So although David does not belong to the house of Saul, because he has now got a covenant with Jonathon he is a member of the family.

A summary

- 1 Samuel 16 David is anointed as king
- 1 Samuel 17, he functions under that anointing by killing the 'strongman'.
- 1 Samuel 18 he enters into a covenant with the son of Saul, thus becoming heir to the promises of the son and can accept the crown in the flesh as well as in the spirit.
- 1 Samuel 19 David marries the daughter of Saul and his inheritance as son in law becomes further established.

Then comes the trial which is after David has been greatly established in the promises. The trial serves to humble David and make him recognize that his kingship is dependent on God, not on man. So although David is anointed king, is strongly attached to the current royal family through 2 covenants (A covenant with Saul's son Jonathan. A covenant of marriage with Saul's daughter Michal), and has the support of the public and the army, his kingdom is dependent on God and this is the part of the relationship that needs forging.

Read 1 Samuel 18 through to chapter 21.

To forge the relationship God does with David what he did with Moses, Abram, and all of those men and women of God, he sends him into exile. David is exiled from the kingdom over which he is anointed king so that the promise is inherited by faith, not by sight.

In 1 Samuel 22 the outcasts gather around David. These become his army. This is a foreshadowing of the kingdom of God where the outcasts gather around Jesus and become a holy army of saints, ***'I came not to call the righteous but sinners to repentance.'(Luke 5:32)***

David becomes king

2 Samuel 1:1,2

"After the death of Saul, David returned from his defeat of the Amalekites and spent two days in Ziklag. On the third day a man came from Saul's camp, with his clothes torn and dirt on his head. Going to David, he fell to the ground in homage."

David knows he is going to be king at this stage because of God's promise. Note the phrase 'on the third day' and a man falls to the ground in front of the anointed one 'in homage'. All of this is a foreshadowing of the Messiah who rises on the third day and enables us to enter into the fulfillment of the promise. At the end of Luke's Gospel the disciples (those from 'Saul's' camp who have entered into the presence of the anointed one) do homage to Jesus just as the man here does homage to David.

Read 2 Samuel 5:1-5. According to verse 2 what did God promise David?

According to verse 5 how long did David reign in Hebron and then in Jerusalem?

This paragraph is of significance. David is called 'King David' at the age of thirty, the same age Jesus begins his public ministry and the same age a Rabbi begins his ministry. He reigns for 40 years which is a time of testing or a generation. This is divided into two elements.

- 7 years and 6 months in Hebron over Judah.

- Thirty three years in Jerusalem over the whole kingdom. Jesus spent thirty three years on earth. David is called the Messianic king because his reign is considered to be a foreshadowing of the Messiah.

Once David has virtually defeated the Philistines he brings the Ark of God into its rightful home at the centre of the Israelite nation. 2 Samuel 6 describes the bringing of the ark from Baala in Judah to Jerusalem. Then in 2 Samuel 7 David wants to build a temple of worship for God. The consequence of this desire in David is the establishing of the covenant between God and the Kingdom of Israel. Read 2 Samuel 7 and write out verses 12-16 which define the covenant:-

According to verse 12 what is God going to do when David's time is finished?

____

What will David's son do and what will God do with the throne?

____

____

Verses 14 and 15 describe the father/son relationship that God wishes to have with everybody. Write it down thinking of your own relationship with God.

____

____

Finally in verse 16 God defines the signs of the covenant that will endure. What are the signs of the covenant?

____

____

These words are the covenant with David. Note that this is not a blood covenant as with David's predecessors, because the blood covenant has been established; now the covenant is by the power of God's Word and the faith of his servants. Note that 2 Samuel 7 begins with the idea of David 'resting'. This takes place in chapter 7, a parallel with the day of rest on the 7th day! This chapter also sees the completion of God's plan for Israel with the establishment of the throne. Thus we have rest, completion, the covenant and the throne.

The sign of the covenant is the throne that will endure:-

Throne

Hebrew = Kisse

Root word – Kese which means

'Full moon'

The sign of the covenant is the 'kisse' which will endure. This is rooted in the Hebrew word for full moon 'kese'. So there is a connection between the throne of the house of David, the kingdom of God and the full moon.

Read Genesis 1:16 and write it below:-

____

The greater light to govern the day is the sun which can be seen in a spiritual sense as the light of God's presence which will govern the eternal day, the beatitude of eternal life. The lesser light to govern the night is the moon which can be seen in a spiritual sense as firstly the nation of Israel, the throne of King David; then the Church, the Kingdom of God on earth, which governs the earth which is in darkness until Jesus returns in glory.

God has achieved his purpose in David's life and now wants to purify him and prepare him for the eternal reward. Thus there is the revelation of personal sin in 2 Samuel 11 when David commits adultery with Bathsheba. Even in this God works his wonders. Bathsheba becomes the mother of Solomon through whom the temple is built, God's wisdom is shown, and the kingdom endures.

Sadly the fruit of David's sin is the kingdom is eventually divided and thus weakened. Once again this is the revelation of God showing us the fruit of sin in contrast to the fruit of holiness. When David was growing in holiness he:-

- established the nation as a kingdom,
- established Jerusalem as the capital,
- brought in the Ark of the Covenant, and
- received the blessing of covenant with God.

Even when David sins God can further his kingdom promises. Read 1 Chronicles 21 Satan attacks the nation of Israel through tempting King David. God gives David a choice of 'chastisements'.

In verse 13 what is David's preference?

____

In verse 15 where is the Angel standing when God tells him to stop the chastisement?

____

What does the Angel tell David to do in verse 18?

____

In verse 26 what does David do and how does God respond?

____

____

Turn to 2 Chronicles 3. Where does Solomon build the Jerusalem temple?

____

The threshing floor is where Ornan the Jebusite used to thresh wheat. This was a process used to separate wheat from chaff. The person threshing would use a threshing sledge to cast the wheat and chaff into the air. The chaff would be blown away in the wind while the heavier wheat would fall back to the floor. After doing this for a while all that would be left would be the wheat. The chaff would be blown away ready to be burnt.

The chaff symbolizes our sin, the wheat symbolizes virtue. By inspiring David to buy the threshing floor of Ornan the Jebusite as the future foundation for the Jerusalem temple God is showing us that he wants this place to be where the wheat is separated from the chaff. This is the place of 'chastisement'.

Read Luke 3:15-17. What does John the Baptist say that Jesus will do in verse 15?

____

In verse 17 what does Jesus do with the winnowing fan?

____

____

Jesus is the one who clears the threshing floor of the chaff (sin) so that only wheat (virtue) remains.

Read John 1:29. What does Jesus, the Lamb of God, do with our sin?

____

The threshing floor that Jesus wants to clear is our soul. We are a living temple. The Holy Spirit is the 'ruach', the breath of God. Jesus sends the breath of God to separate the wheat from the chaff. Then he sends the fire on us to burn up the chaff and leave just the wheat.

Daily meditations and readings:-
Meditations Readings

Day one: Hebrews 11:33 1 Samuel 16
Day two: Hebrews 12:2 1 Samuel 20
Day three Psalm 51:3 Psalm 89
Day four: Psalm 51:13 Psalm 116
Day five: Acts 2:25 Acts 2
Day six: Wisdom 3:1 Sirach 47
Day seven: Wisdom 6:12 Acts 13

9. Jesus – his early life and public ministry

Read Philippians 2:5-11 and write out verse 6:-

____

Jesus emptied himself, taking the form of a slave. He **was** and **is** the Son of God, but laid down his Sonship and functioned under the Abrahamic covenant in order to redeem those under sin. He 'removes his cloak' of his Sonship, takes upon himself our humanity, so that we can lose our sin and become songs and daughters of God. We can call this the Covenant exchange.

From the Mass:

'By the mystery of this water and wine

may we come to share in the divinity of Christ,

who humbled himself to share in our humanity.'

Key stages in the life of Christ

Read *Luke 2:21 – 24*, The Covenant of circumcision and consecration of the first born.

What is done to Jesus in verse 21?

____

____

And as the first born in verse 23?

____

Jesus was born and ministered under the Abrahamic covenant. His entire ministry was performed under the 'old covenant' until the sacrifice on the cross.

Read Luke 2:41-52, Possibly his Bar Mitzvah

What does Jesus say to his parents in verse 49?

____

____

Read Luke 3:16. What does John the Baptist say Jesus will do?

____

____

Jesus is the one who baptises us. Although a priest may perform the baptism ceremony, he is doing it in 'persona Christi;' in the person of Christ, he is acting on Christ's behalf. Thus although the priest is doing the physical ceremony, the baptism is performed by Jesus Christ.

The baptism of Jesus

Read Luke 3:21-22. Write out verse 21

____

____

What does God the Father say in verse 22?

____

____

Up to this point in history, since Adam and Eve left Eden, heaven had been closed. Because Jesus humbles himself and accepts that which is necessary for sinful man, the heavens are finally opened and the Father's voice can be clearly heard. He speaks of His Son.

It is said that God has only spoken one word – 'Jesus'.

Jesus is baptised by John, the last prophet of the old covenant and considered to be the last High Priest. Jesus accepts baptism to fulfil the law.

Note that Jesus is 'about thirty' when he is baptised and ready to begin his public ministry. As previously mentioned this is the same age at which David became King, it was also the same age at which a Jewish man could become a Rabbi.

Luke 4:1-13 Jesus suffers temptation defeating it by the Word of God.

What does Satan show Jesus in verses 5?

____

____

According to verse 6 how did Satan come into possession of the above?

____

As a result of original sin the whole world has fallen into the power of the evil one. Jesus has not come to wrestle the world from Satan's power but to establish his own kingdom. A kingdom that is 'in the world but not of the world' (John 17;14-16)

Jesus begins his public ministry.

Read Luke 4:18-19. What has Jesus been anointed to do?

____

____

____

Jesus was proclaiming a 'year of jubilee' which is from Leviticus 25. It is the most wonderful year in ancient Israel and has four aspects to it:-

- All debts are cancelled
- All slaves are set free
- All property is returned to its rightful owner
- A year of rest

Each of the above four aspects corresponds with the four dimensions of Jesus first public proclamation of the Torah.

- 'Glad tidings to the poor' are the cancellation of debts. Our greatest debt is sin which leaves us in abject spiritual poverty. This is cancelled by the cross of Jesus.
- 'Liberty to captives' is the setting free of slaves. Sin has left us as slaves to Satan's dominion of the world. Jesus sets us free from slavery to Satan through his death and resurrection.
- 'Recovery of sight to the blind' is the return of property to its rightful owner. Sin has left mankind blind to the glory of God's kingdom. God wants to restore this kingdom to our hearts and in order to do this he needs to open our eyes to its glories. Jesus does this by his atoning death on the cross.
- 'Let the oppressed go free' is a year of rest. Work can be oppressive and man's greatest oppression is sin. Man works hard to save himself from life's ills. Jesus comes, dies, rises, and sets man free from the oppressive labour of sin. We are saved by grace and can rest in God's grace. (cf. Hebrews 4).

The essence of the ministry of Jesus Christ is to set humanity free from the power of sin and the dominance of Satan. This is done by removing sin and establishing the kingdom of light. All of this is achieved through his passion, death and resurrection. This sermon at Nazareth, coming straight after his baptism and the temptation in the wilderness, sets the scene for his public ministry.

Read Acts 10:38. What is Jesus anointed with and what is the purpose?

____

____

Write out Hebrews 2:14.

____

____

Read Matthew 5:1-17, the Beatitudes.

As Moses delivered the law on Mt. Sinai, so Jesus delivers the new law the covenant of love, on the Mount of the Beatitudes. Fr Richard Rohr calls these the 'happy attitudes'. Write out the complete beatitude below opposite the beginning part.

Blessed are the poor in spirit

____

Blessed are the gentle

____

Blessed are those who mourn

____

Blessed are those who hunger and thirst for righteousness

____

Blessed are the merciful

____

Blessed are the pure in heart

____

Blessed are the peacemakers

____

Blessed are those who are persecuted in the cause of righteousness

____

Blessed are you when people abuse you, and persecute you and speak all kinds of calumny against you falsely on my account

____

Each beatitude contains an incredible amount of teaching. The one worth mentioning at this point is the poor in spirit. As previously mentioned, we are poor in spirit. We are so poverty stricken there are no words to convey the miserable state we find ourselves in due to sin. Poor beyond measure, blind, naked, wounded, deaf, and bloodied. Jesus enters fully into this human condition and takes it fully upon himself. He shares in our poverty so that we can share in his riches. He took our sin upon himself so that we can receive fully his righteousness.

This exchange of Jesus taking upon himself our human condition and our partaking in his divine state is all seen in his public ministry through healing, deliverance and the forgiveness of sins.

Read Luke 4:31-44.

What is the man set free from?

____

What does Jesus do at the home of Simon's mother in law?

____

These are both signs of the coming of the kingdom of God.

Who is my neighbour? - The Good Samaritan. Luke 10:29-35

In many circles this parable is greatly misunderstood in today's world. However, the great theologian and Father of the Church Origen (born 185 A.D.) showed us how Jesus is the Good Samaritan. Humanity is 'the man'.

"Because he wished to justify himself, he said to Jesus, "And who is my neighbor?" Jesus replied, "A man fell victim to robbers as he went down from Jerusalem to Jericho. They stripped and beat him and went off leaving him half-dead. A priest happened to be going down that road, but when he saw him, he passed by on the opposite side. Likewise a Levite came to the place, and when he saw him, he passed by on the opposite side. But a Samaritan traveler who came upon him was moved with compassion at the sight. He approached the victim, poured oil and wine over his wounds and bandaged them. Then he lifted him up on his own animal, took him to an inn and cared for him. The next day he took out two silver coins and gave them to the innkeeper with the instruction, 'Take care of him. If you spend more than what I have given you, I shall repay you on my way back.'

Here is an interpretation provided by Origen.

'A man' in Hebrew is 'Adam'. Thus Adam fell victim to robbers. The robber is Satan (John 10:10). Adam is on his way from the God's holy city (Jerusalem/Eden) to Jericho (the cursed place – Joshua 6:17). Jericho is a sign of sin. Adam fell from Eden to sin and fell victim to Satan. He was stripped of grace, and left half dead, the consequences of sin. We have lost relationship with God and are 'dead in sin'.

Neither the priest nor the Levite has the means to restore humanity so they avoid the issue of sin; only the Samaritan traveller can help the man. This is Jesus. The Samaritans were outcasts as was Jesus. Jesus was a traveler. He had no place to rest his head.

Jesus approaches the victim – he approaches humanity which is dead in sin.

He pours oil – Jesus pours out the Holy Spirit.

He pours wine – Jesus gives us the new wine of the new covenant, his precious blood.

He lifts him up on his own animal. The Greek word means a beast of burden. Jesus is the one who takes our burdens upon himself.

The inn is the church, the innkeeper is the Pope

The two silver coins symbolise the sacraments of the Eucharist, the body and blood of Christ which Christ gives to the church so it can take care of its members. With these sacraments the church can heal our wounds and tend to us.

And Christ declares 'Take care of him, I will repay you on my return'

Read Luke 13:10-17

How many times is the word 'sabbath' is used in this passage?

____

Jesus performed several miracles on the Sabbath as a sign of the salvation that he offers where we can rest from our meager efforts at trying to achieve our own salvation and simply receive the free gift offered in Jesus.

Write down verse 16.

____

The reference to 'daughter of Abraham' is pointing out that this woman is in covenant with God through Abraham, yet is held in bondage to Satan through the infirmity. To Jesus this is an unacceptable circumstance. The Sabbath is the perfect day on which to set her free but sadly the Pharisaical law at the time approached the Sabbath in a very legalistic manner which allowed animals to be fed and waters but not people to be healed and set free.

This woman was set free through the power of God available to man through the Abrahamic covenant. The new covenant in the blood of Jesus has not yet been established. All of these miracles and healings are being performed through the covenant of circumcision.

There are four different aspects to the ministry of Jesus:-

- Proclamation of the Good News of the Kingdom of God
- Healing of the sick

- Forgiveness of sins
- Deliverance from evil spirits.

These are all still evidenced in the Church today, 20 centuries later. However, whereas the Gospels have more emphasis on proclamation, healing, deliverance and forgiveness, the church can tend to focus on a different order; proclamation, forgiveness, healing, and occasionally but sadly not enough, deliverance from evil spirits.

Jesus walking in obedience to the Father

Read John 5:19. What does Jesus say about his relationship with God the Father?

____

Write out John 5:30

____

Write out John 8:28

____

Finally write out John 14:10

____

____

Everything that Jesus said and did came from his Father. He only spoke what his Father gave him to say, he only did what he saw his Father doing. Jesus did nothing independent of his heavenly Father. Neither should we. In fact, if we walk in the same ways that Jesus walks in.

Read John 14:12. What does Jesus say about those who believe in him?

____

Jesus functioned under the Abrahamic covenant, we have a better covenant to function under; we function under the new and everlasting covenant in the blood of Jesus Christ.

Daily meditations and readings:-
Meditations Readings
Day one: Philippians 2:5 Philippians 2
Day two: Luke 2:51 Luke 1
Day three: Luke 4:8 Luke 4
Day four: Luke 10:20 Matthew 5 and 6
Day five: John 5:19 Matthew 7
Day six: John 14:1 John 1
Day seven: John 15:12 John 6

10. Jesus, a covenant with the world.

Read John 13.

This is one of those very familiar passages of scripture that is read out in Churches all over the world every year on Maundy Thursday. Consequently we can miss out on the meaning of what Jesus is teaching us because we are familiar with the passage.

What is Jesus fully aware of in verse 3?

____

____

This makes Jesus the most powerful person alive, and he knows it. Yet instead of taking the 'power position', Jesus does what we may consider to be the exact opposite course of action; he washes his disciples feet. He takes off his outer garment and assumes the position of the household slave. This was traditionally the person who would wash the feet of everybody who is entering into the household. Thus before a person could enter the upper room where Jesus was gathered with his disciples, somebody should have washed all the feet. This did not happen until Jesus adopted the position of the slave. To a normal Jew this would be a difficult thing to accept, but for the disciples to allow their 'Rabbi' to do this is extraordinary. It goes against all normal convention and there is nothing in modern culture that would convey the message appropriately because we do not necessarily have the full understanding of what it means to be a slave.

As Jesus approaches Simon Peter the latter refuses to have his feet washed. Jesus makes a firm reply.

What does Jesus say to him (verse 8)?

____

____

Jesus is telling Peter that unless he cleans him then Peter cannot enter into the kingdom of God. Consider that the household slave enables the visitors to enter into the household by cleaning their feet. Jesus has taken that position and unless he cleans us of our sin we cannot enter into the household of God.

Depending on the translation Jesus says to Peter 'You can have no inheritance with me'. The Greek word for 'inheritance' is

Meros

Which means

'Portion'

Jesus is saying to Peter that if he does not let Jesus wash him he will not enter into heavenly glory (this is our portion or inheritance). This makes perfect sense. If we do not let Jesus wash us, sanctify us; make us holy, we cannot enter into heaven.

Write out Philippians 2:7.

____

____

Jesus then declares that his disciples are clean, though not all of them are. This is because for three years Jesus has been teaching his disciples the Word of God which is equivalent to a spiritual bath.

Read Ephesians 5:26. What does it say about the Word and washing?

____

____

In some translations it talks about a 'bath of water with the word'. If we immerse ourselves in God's Word it is like a 'spiritual' bath of water.

What does Jesus tell his disciples (us) to do in verse 14?

Jesus then teaches his disciples the final lesson in this particular scenario. He has washed his disciples which is a sign, a foreshadowing, a symbol, of his cleansing us from sin. Once he has done this he then gives them a command.

What does Jesus tell his disciples to do in verse 14?

This means that he no longer wants us to gossip about each other, envy one another's gifts, fight over gifts; sin against one another. Quite the opposite! Jesus is telling us to cleanse one another from sin. He wants us to help each other grow in holiness.

Read Colossians 3:13. What does St Paul tell us to do?

John 14:1-3

"Do not let your hearts be troubled. You have faith in God; have faith also in me. In my Father's house there are many dwelling places. If there were not, would I have told you that I am going to prepare a place for you? And if I go and prepare a place for you, I will come back again and take you to myself, so that where I am you also may be.

These are the same words that a Hebrew male would speak to the woman he has chosen, or who has been chosen for him, as his future bride. They are taken from the betrothal ceremony and would have been spoken by St Joseph to Our Lady before she conceived Jesus. At this point Jesus is speaking them first to his Apostles, then to his church, us. We should find reassurance that Jesus has not only prepared a place for us in his and our Father's house, but that Jesus is going to lead us to that place and prepare our hearts for the Kingdom. It is Jesus who sanctifies us.

As stated in the first session on the marriage covenant:-

Betrothal

Hebrew – Kiddushim

Comes from the Hebrew word

Kadosh - Holy

The implication being that being 'holy' means being betrothed to God. A bit like being engaged means you can no longer date other people, you are preparing for marriage when you will belong to one person, your spouse. You are holy unto your future spouse.

Read John 15:12-17
What is the new commandment Jesus gives to his followers?

How does Jesus define the greatest love?

The measure of love that Jesus gives us here is not to do with the amount of pleasure you can give or receive from another person, it is the amount you are willing to sacrifice for another. Jesus provides us with the benchmark. We make ourselves enemies of God through our sin, but Jesus wants us to be his friends and is willing to lay down his life for his enemy in order to make that enemy, us, his friend.

What does Jesus ask his friends to do?

And what is the command he asks us to obey?

The disciples of Jesus have a very simple commandment to obey. The consequences of this commandment are very powerful and found in 1 John 4:12.

What is the consequence of our loving one another?

____

Return to John 15:15. Why does Jesus call us friends?

____

Jesus tells us that he can call us his friends because he has made known to us everything he has learned from his Father. Think about the people or person you regard as a friend and how much personal information you would trust them with. Jesus takes this human attribute and applies it to his relationship with us. He makes known to us everything he has learned and that is a measure of his friendship, a complete and total commitment. Jesus does not hold back.

Read Luke 22:14-20, the last supper, the memorial meal, the covenant meal. What does Jesus say in verse 19:-

____

The Greek word for 'remember' or 'remembrance' (depending on the translation you are reading) does not mean to 'remember' as if the event is in the past and is far distant. The Greek word is 'anamnesis' which has the meaning to relive as if you were actually there. Thus when Catholics celebrate the Mass it is not so much a case of remembering an event that took place 2000 years ago. It is about us reliving the last supper and Calvary; they become present to us, or alternatively, we become present to them. We go back to Calvary. It is 'now'.

What does Jesus say in verse 20?

____

This verse is very familiar to Catholics so we can 'skip' over it without realising the enormity of what is being said. Jesus is establishing a new covenant with us. Unlike the other covenants with Adam, Noah, Abraham, Moses and David, this one is not being established through the killing of an innocent animal. This one is being established through Jesus shedding His own blood. Thus the promises are greater because the cost is so high. If a person made covenant through their own sacrifice we may pay attention to the sacrifice that was necessary. However, this covenant is being made through the blood of God. It is far superior to the covenants of the past and thus the promises are also far superior. The covenants of the past almost focussed on temporal promises (the land of Canaan, no more flooding of the land, etc). This covenant focuses on an eternal kingdom in which we are invited to live.

During the celebration of Mass the bread becomes flesh through the power of the words and that it is the action of Christ. When the priest speaks 'this is my body' the bread becomes the flesh of Jesus Christ. When the priest speaks 'this is my blood' the wine becomes the blood of Jesus Christ. The priest speaks these words and those words carry the power of God.

> It is not man that causes the things offered to become the Body and Blood of Christ, but he who was crucified for us, Christ himself. The priest, in the role of Christ, pronounces these words, but their power and grace are God's. 'This is my body', he says. This word transforms the things offered.'[75]

Flesh and blood
Read 1 Corinthian 11:23-32
In Verse 27 what does St Paul say about a person who receives the body and blood unworthily?

____

What happens to these people according to verses 29 and 30?

____

Many people want to approach and receive the Lord's body and blood regardless of their lifestyle. Some people want to live their lives the way they want to, not to follow the guidance and teaching of the Catholic Church, yet they want to receive the Eucharist even though their lives are not in communion with 'Rome'. This behaviour is not acceptable to God and can bring a person under condemnation as God, through the power of the Holy Spirit revealed to Saint Paul in this verse. If somebody is living an immoral life but receives the Eucharist they come under their own condemnation because they do not recognise the sacredness of what they are consuming. By refusing such people the Eucharist the church is protecting them from their own foolish behaviour.

Read Leviticus 17:11, 14. What does verse 11 say about blood?

____

What does verse 14 say about blood?

____

Read John 6:53. What does Jesus say about his flesh and blood?

____

Again in verse 54, what does a person have who eats his flesh and drinks his blood?

____

What are the consequences of eating his flesh and drinking his blood in verse 56?

____

Three times Jesus tells us to eat his flesh and drink his blood in order for us to have life within us, and there in the book of Leviticus Jesus tells us three times that blood is the seat of life.

So why does Jesus tell us in John 6 to eat his flesh and drink his blood, yet in Leviticus he tells us not to drink blood. One of the things that the 'law' or 'Torah' does is to reveal the nature of sin, that sin kills; sin leads to death. The life of every creature is in the creature's blood, and as every creature is subject to the kingdom of darkness and thus to death, then the blood of every creature carries death. Sin, sickness and disease are all carried in blood. However, when Jesus comes he is free from sin and its effects so by eating his flesh and drinking his blood the opposite takes place; we receive life.

The passion of Jesus

Luke 22:39-46. The garden of Gethsemane,

"Then going out he went, as was his custom, to the Mount of Olives, and the disciples followed him. When he arrived at the place he said to them, "Pray that you may not undergo the test." After withdrawing about a stone's throw from them and kneeling, he prayed, saying, "Father, if you are willing, take this cup away from me; still, not my will but yours be done." (And to strengthen him an angel from heaven appeared to him. He was in such agony and he prayed so fervently that his sweat became like drops of blood falling on the ground.) When he rose from prayer and returned to his disciples, he found them sleeping from grief. He said to them, "Why are you sleeping? Get up and pray that you may not undergo the test."

The word Gethesemane consists of:-

Gath = wine

Shemen = oil

The two words combine to

Produce 'wine and oil press.'

This takes place on the Mount of Olives where the full anointing of his ministry comes down on him for him to fulfil his call to destroy the power of sin. His agony, the full weight of the covenant is on him, blood flows due to the stress of sin coming down on Jesus.

Covenant –

'To cut where <u>blood flows</u>'

Read Matthew 27:16-26

What is the name of the murderer?

____

What does Exodus 12:5 say about choosing an animal for the Passover?

____

The murderer is called (Jesus) Barabbas. This name can be broken into several constituent parts.

Jesus – 'God Saves'

Bar – Son of

Abba – Father (daddy)

Thus Jesus, the Messiah, the true son of the Father, the sheep, is standing in one place. Next to him is stood Jesus, the murderer, also the 'son of the father' (Barabbas). Jesus our Saviour is the sheep, Jesus Barabbas is the goat. The Jews choose their Passover victim.

In a sense we are the murderer, we are the ones whose sin took Jesus to the cross. We are stood in front of the seat of judgement where Pilate places us next to the Son of God. Every time is the same. Jesus, the Son of God, is chosen to take our place of punishment. He dies for our sins. He dies so that we may live.

Covenant terms from the cross

Whilst in the agony of suffering the awful death of crucifixion, Jesus speaks seven phrases from the cross. Write them below next to the scripture references.

Luke 23:34 ____

Luke 23:43 ____

Mark 15:34 ____

John 19:26, 27 ____

Luke 23:46 ____

John 19:28 ____

John 19:30 ____

In John 19:34 the soldier thrusts a lance into the side of Christ and Blood and water flowed out.

Covenant –

'To cut where blood flows'.

"Dying you destroyed our death,

Rising you restored our life

Lord Jesus come in glory"

After his death Jesus descends into hell and preaches the Gospel to the souls in prison.

'Jesus did not descend into hell to deliver the damned, nor to destroy the hell of damnation, but to free the just who had gone before him.'[76]

Read Isaiah 53:4-6, the suffering servant. In verse 4 what was Jesus carrying or bearing that was ours?

____

In verse 5 what was Jesus doing for us?

____

____

In verse 6 what did God bring upon him?

____

In verse 5 is the word describing healing past, present or future tense? (ie we 'were healed', 'will be healed', or 'are healed')?

____

When Jesus died on the cross he healed us of our sin and our sicknesses, which are the fruit of sin. However, because his death is for all sins, past, present and future, the healing happened when the fall took place because it is appropriated by faith. In other words, even though Elijah did not see Jesus die, he could enter into salvation because he believed that God would and could set him free from sin. The same applies to Enoch in the book of Genesis.

The penalty for eating from the tree of the knowledge of good and evil is death; the penalty for sin is death. Jesus takes our sin upon himself; dies on our behalf, defeats death by rising from the dead, then gives us His life.

Read John 1:29. What does John the Baptist say about Jesus?

____

Read John 1:31. What was the purpose of John's baptism?

____

John was the son of Elizabeth and Zechariah. They were of Aaron's line which makes John of the High Priesthood line. He is considered by some to be the last High Priest of the Old Covenant. When he baptises Jesus he is passing on the mantle of High Priest to his cousin. John is the High Priest who prepares the sacrificial lamb to take away the sins of the world.

Why Jesus?

Colossians 1:15-20

"He is the image of the invisible God, the firstborn of all creation. For in him were created all things in heaven and on earth, the visible and the invisible, whether thrones or dominions or principalities or powers; all things were created through him and for him. He is before all things, and in him all things hold together. He is the head of the body, the church. He is the beginning, the firstborn from the dead, that in all things he himself might be preeminent. For in him all the fullness was pleased to dwell, and through him to reconcile all things for him, making peace by the blood of his cross (through him), whether those on earth or those in heaven."

How should we respond?

Colossians 3:1, 2

"If then you were raised with Christ, seek what is above, where Christ is seated at the right hand of God. Think of what is above, not of what is on earth. For you have died, and your life is hidden with Christ in God. When Christ your life appears, then you too will appear with him in glory."

If you have not yet done it, this is an opportunity for you to renew your commitment to Christ. Now that you have a great understanding of the biblical covenants and quite possibly a different understanding of your relationship with Christ, it is ideal for you to welcome him into your heart and ask him to renew your relationship with you.

Read Revelation 3:20. What is Jesus doing and what does he want to do?

____

Jesus stands at the door of our heart waiting to be invited in so he can share a rich banquet with us. Invite him in and spend a moment with him in the silence of your heart.

11. Your Righteousness in Christ

Read Matthew 6:20, 21 and 33.
What does Matthew 6:33 say about righteousness and the kingdom of God?

____

Righteousness is something quite extraordinary that we don't necessarily grasp very well as Catholics. The majority of us will probably believe quite freely that we are wretched sinners, going to purgatory, and will carry a burden of guilt with us for a long time. However, this is not living the way Christ wants us to live.

Another problem we may have is because we are immersed in a world that is incredibly materialistic, we can be influenced by it. However, Jesus tells us not to seek the things of the world. That is equal to setting our hearts on these things. He tells us to 'seek first' something quite different – the Kingdom of God.

Righteousness

Referring to some of the scriptures we have studied in this workbook.

Read Genesis 6:9. How does it describe Noah?

____

What does Genesis 15:6 say that God 'credited' to Abram?

____

Read Job 4:17. What does it say about 'man' or 'a mortal'?

____

In Psalm 146:8 who does the Lord love?

____

Write out Proverbs 11:11

____

Write out the prophecy of Jeremiah 23:5 regarding the Messiah

____

In Matthew 5:6 Jesus talks about those who hunger and thirst. What do they hunger and thirst for?

____

In Matthew 5:10, who is given the kingdom of Heaven?

____

In the above scriptures you may have read 'upright', 'good', or 'righteous'. The latter would probably be more accurate. What is righteousness?

We may think that righteousness is to do with our conduct, but this is not necessarily so. Biblically, righteousness is more to do with relationship than conduct. God is the only righteous one, as He is the only holy one, the only good one. Nobody else is good, or righteous, or holy. These are attributes that God gives to us in order for us to enter into relationship with Him. One could say that they are the attributes of the family of God. If we want to belong to that family, which would be a wise thing, we need these attributes. We cannot 'get' them; they are freely given to us.

Righteousness can mean 'right standing'. It suggests that although we do wrong things, God chooses not to count those wrong things against us, but bestows righteousness on us. This means that we are in right standing with God. It could be viewed as the relationship between a father and son. The son does something that seriously damages the relationship and it means he cannot enter into his father's presence for fear of being punished. However, the father prefers the son to enter into his presence because of his love for him. His love overrides the negative action of the son.

The act of entering into the presence of the father is called 'right standing', or righteousness. Although the son has committed 'a sin', the father chooses not to count that sin against him and instead bestows 'righteousness' on him so that they can have fellowship.

For us and our relationship with God, we commit sin which severely fractures our relationship with God. In order to repair the damage Jesus dies, rises, and ascends to His Father. When we are baptised it is into His death and resurrection it is no longer I who live. My baptism was into the death of Christ. When Christ rose I rose 'with him and in him' so that it is not longer me who is living, it is Christ living in me. This is a covenant exchange. When I come into God's presence through prayer it is not I who the Father is seeing, it is Christ. This is why all of our prayers are made 'In Jesus name'.

Although our conduct may not be good, our relationship is!

Another way of looking at righteousness is this. Imagine the King's Court from the Middle Ages in England. You are a peasant. You want justice because of some wrong that has been committed against you and in order to secure justice you have to speak to the King. However, if you enter into the King's presence and speak you are committing high treason and will die. Nonetheless, that is the only way. You go to the palace and enter into the King's presence on your knees with your head down. You are not allowed to look at the King or stand in his presence at this stage. The King sees you and points his royal sceptre at you. This action of the King gives you authority to speak. It means that the King has put you on equal standing with him, alternatively known as 'righteousness'. You have righteousness in the mind of the King, granted by him, which means you can stand in his presence and petition him for justice.

God is the great King. He pointed His sceptre at us through Jesus and we have been granted 'righeousness'. We can speak freely and petition God for justice.

Read Esther 4:11. What happens if a person approaches the King without being summoned?

What does the King have to do to spare them from death?

The next scripture may be difficult to find depending on the translation you are using.
Read Esther 5/D12 and write it below. It should refer to the golden sceptre.

These scriptures show clearly the scenario that ruled in the King's courts for many years. If a person approached without permission they could be killed. Only by the pointing of the golden sceptre did the King spare their life and the person could petition the King.

The Jews understood this principle and God gave them the Holy of Holies within the temple of worship as a means of approaching God. This is because of sin. Sin separated us from God and the consequence was that we do not have 'righteousness'. It is not possible for man to approach God by his own volition. We need, or we needed, somebody to destroy the power of sin which had separated us from God.

The price of sin was death (If you eat from the tree of knowledge of good and evil you will die – Gen. 2:17). Man ate from that tree and died. He fell into disobedience, separated himself from God, and can no longer walk in the presence of God. In order to repair the damage and restore us into right relationship with God a man has to pay the price for all of humanity.

The Old Testament system of sacrifices had the purpose of atoning for sins. However, this only meant that sin was 'covered' (atone means 'to cover'). When Jesus died and rose again he appeared before the Father and obtained forgiveness for sins. The death and resurrection of Jesus Christ cancelled the debt of sin. Jesus is the man who paid the full price for the sin of all humanity, past, present and future. He died so that we could live.

Read 2 Cor. 5:17. Write it out below.

Consider that before Christ very few people had the grace of righeousness. Noah, Shem, Abraham, Isaac, Jacob, Moses, and a few others. However, this is not the way God wants it.

Read Isaiah 45:8. Write it out below:-

This scripture speaks of righteousness and salvation pouring down from the heavens like rain and producing much fruit. This is what happened after the death, resurrection and ascension of Jesus Christ.

> The grace of the Holy Spirit confers upon us the righteousness of God. Uniting us by faith and baptism to the Passion and Resurrection of Christ, the Spirit makes us sharers in his life.[77]

> Like conversion, justification has two aspects. Moved by grace, man turns towards God and away from sin, and so accepts forgiveness and righteousness from on high.[78]

Justification

Like righteousness this is another Christian word that can be difficult to understand or comprehend.

> The grace of the Holy Spirit has the power to justify us, that is, to cleanse us from our sins and to communicate to us 'the righteousness of God through faith in Jesus Christ' and through baptism.[79]

Righteousness is about our standing with God. It means we can talk to God and walk with him even though we have sin in us.

Justification is about the cleansing of sins. One could say that although we sin, God treats me 'just if I'd' (justified) never done it! This is a very accurate way of thinking. Once I have confessed my sins in the confessional, all of my sins belong on the cross. They no longer belong to me. They have been removed.

Read John 1:29. What does the Lamb of God do?

Now write out Romans 10:8

The Lamb of God has removed our sins. Like the waste disposal people who remove the rubbish from our streets, Christ has removed the sin. He took it on his body, nailing it to the cross, and when he died, all of humanity's sin, my sin, your sin, it all died with him. Every sin in the past, present and future all died with Christ.

When a person is baptised they are 'immersed' (baptised) into the death of Jesus Christ. Their sin dies at this point. When they come out of the water they are 'in Christ'. They are part of his body. Everybody who is baptised is like this. We all belong to the Body of Christ.

At this point we receive from God graces necessary for our continued relationship with Him:-

- Righteousness so we can talk to God
- Justification so we are cleansed from sin
- Sanctification so we can grow in holiness
- Redemption, we have been brought and paid for by the blood of Christ.

These are all freely given by God to the believer.

God gave himself to us through his Spirit. By the participation of the Spirit, we become communicants in the divine nature...For this reason, those in whom the Spirit dwells are divinized.[80]

When explaining divinization, Thomas Aquinas used the example of an iron poker heated in a fire. Though the red-hot poker never itself becomes fire, yet it participates in every characteristic of the fire. So do we participate in the divine nature through the perfection brought about in purgation[8] and the sacraments. Through these active experiences of the Divine, we are filled to the capacity of our being with divinity.[81]

Justification is the most excellent work of God's love made manifest in Christ Jesus and granted by the Holy Spirit. It is the opinion of St Augustine that 'the justification of the wicked is a greater work than the creation of heaven and earth,' because 'heaven and earth will pass away but the salvation and justification of the elect...will not pass away.'

He also holds that the justification of sinners surpasses the creation of the angels in justice, in that it bears witness to a greater mercy.[82]

This workbook began by showing that God's original plan for humanity was similar to a marital relationship. Humanity broke that relationship by rejecting God's plan and choosing self. Over the centuries God has been speaking into humanity's mess and reconciling the world to himself through His Son. He has been restoring that which was lost so that the New Testament authors can proclaim a new message. We are indeed 'divinized', we are children of God. We are made new in Christ Jesus.

Read the first letter of St John, chapter 3 verses 2 and 3. What does it say we are?

____

What does it say about what we shall be?

____

Read St Paul's first letter to the Corinthians, chapter 13, verse 12. What does it say about how 'we shall see' and 'knowing'?

____

We are already God's children. We shall be transformed into something more glorious when Christ returns in glory because we will be completely sinless. We cannot see God clearly in this life because of our sinful nature, but we will one day, if we persevere, see him face to face. For us to see God face to face he will need to completely transform us so that we become 'like him' - divinized.

Read Colossians 2:1-14. According to verse 14 what has Christ done for you?

---

8.   http://bridegroompress.com/sc/purgat.htm

According to verse 6 what should in whom should we live our lives?

Finally, read Colossians 3:1-3. Where have we been raised to?

As a consequence of this what should our thoughts be on according to verse 2?

According to verse 3 what has happened to me (you) and who is living in us?

This last line is really the essence of what it means to be a Christian in covenant with God. It means that as Christians we can no longer live our lives as we 'want' to. We should learn how God wants us to live by reading the scriptures daily if possible, and behave accordingly. It means that we can no longer live selfishly but must learn to die daily to self so that we can live daily for God.

This is truly living. Not living for self, but living for another. The great exchange is that as we live for God, he lives for us. As we learn to die daily to self so that God can live in us, we learn how wonderful was the sacrifice Jesus made, to die for us so that we can truly be alive.

This is because Jesus came for a specific purpose.

Read John 10:10. Why did Jesus come?

In order for us to have life to the full we must learn to die to our selfish motives and behaviour and live in accordance with God's Word. This is truly living. God living in me means that I am fully alive.

That, surely, is what it means to be Christian, God fully alive in me so that I may be fully alive.

Bibliography

I have referred to Judaism several times in this workbook. Some of the quotes are from sources quoted, others have not been quoted. These are usually from seminars that I have attended over the years where I have not got the source material. However, a visit to a variety of websites will provide the information I used here. I recommend the following:

The centre for Judaic-Christian Studies. http://jcstudies.com/

www.jewishencyclopaedia.com

All Scripture quotations taken from *The New American Bible*, Catholic Study Edition, unless otherwise stated.

Catechism of the Catholic Church, Chapman 1994. Abbreviated as CCC.

Whenever I have referred to the original Hebrew or Greek translations of the Bible I have used:-

STRONG, James, S.T.D., L.L.D. Strong's Exhaustive Concordance of the Bible. World

Bible Publishers, Iowa Falls, Ia. 1993.

FLANNERY, AUSTIN, O.P., *Vatican Council II,* New York: Costello Publishing Company, New Revised Edition 1992. First published 1975.

Documents quoted; *Lumen Gentium and Dei Verbum.*

BOOKER, RICHARD. *The Miracle of the Scarlet Thread.* Destiny Image Publishers, Shippensburg, PA. USA. 1981.

BUCKINGHAM, JAMIE, *A Way Through the Wilderness,* Kingsway Publications,

Eastbourne. 1983

CARROLL, ANNE, *Christ the King, the Lord of History*. Tan Publishers, Ilinois.

First edition 1976. Reprint 1994

GREENBERG, RABBI IRVING, *The Jewish Way, Living the Holidays*, New York: Simon and Schuster, 1993.

HAHN, DR SCOTT, Ph.D., *A Father Who Keeps His Promises*, Ann Arbor, Michigan: Servant Publications, 1998.

MONK, RABBI MICHAEL, *The Wisdom in the Hebrew Alphabet*, New York: Mesorah Publications Ltd., 2010.

OTT, DR LUDWIG, *Fundamentals of Catholic Dogma,* Rockford, Illinois: Tan books and publishers, Inc. 1960. First published 1955.

PILKINGTON, C. M., *Judaism*, London: Hodder & Stoughton, 1995.

POPE JOHN PAUL II. *Novo Millennion Inneunte*. Apostolic Letter, downloaded from www.vatican.va.

POPE JOHN PAUL II, *The Theology of the Body,* Pauline Books and Media,

Boston. 1997

The Kolbe Center for the Study of Creation. 952 Kelly Road, Mt. Jackson, VA 22842.

www.kolbecenter.org

WARKULWIZ, Rev. Victor P. *The Doctrines of Genesis 1-11*. The Missionary Priests

of the Blessed Sacrament. Publication sponsored by Kolbe Centre Center for the Study of Creation, Mount Jackson. VA. 2007.

Zenit News Agency, www.zenit.org

All material contained in this workbook is copyright © Derek Williams 2012.
Derek is a Catholic Evangelist whose principle ministry is to teach the Word of God in the power of the Spirit.

[1] DV, Para. 11.

[2] www.zenit.org, April 25 2007.

[3] *Ibid.,* September 16, 2005.

[4] CCC, Article 2653.

[5] Booker, Richard, The Miracle of the Scarlet Thread, Shippensburg, PA: Destiny Image Publishers, 1981, p.27

[6] John Paul II, The Theology of the Body, Boston: Pauline Books and Media, 1997, p.355.

[7] *Ibid.*

[8] *Ibid.,* p.354.

[9] Ott, Dr Ludwig, Fundamentals of Catholic Dogma, Rockford, Illinois: Tan Books and Publishers, Inc., fourth edition, May 1960, p.468.

[10] http://www.peacepilgrim.com/, 19/4/2012. Alternatively just Google 'Medjugorje marriage ritual'.

[11] CCC, Article 1375.

[12] Ott, Dr Ludwig, Fundamentals of Catholic Dogma. Rockford, Illinois: Tan Books and Publishers, Inc., fourth edition, May 1960, p.468.

[13] Booker, Richard. The Miracle of the Scarlet Thread, Shippensburg, PA: Destiny Image Publishers, 1981, p.27

[14] *Ibid.,* p.28.

[15] http://www.spurgeon.org/sermons/0976.htm. 19/4/2012.

[16] http://en.wikipedia.org/wiki/Treaty_of_Windsor_(1386), 19/4/2012.

[17] These insights were derived from various written and spoken sources down the years. However, if you visit www.judaism.com, you will find information about 'Ketubah', and 'Huppah' and can read up on Judaism.

[18] Booker, Richard, The Miracle of the Scarlet Thread, Shippensburg, PA: Destiny Image Publishers, 1981, p.27

[19] *Ibid.,* p.28.

[20] *Ibid.*

[21] Booker, Richard, The Miracle of the Scarlet Thread, Shippensburg, PA: Destiny Image Publishers, 1981, p.29.

[22] *Ibid.*

[23] http://www.tithebarns.co.uk/

[24] www.wikipedia.org

[25] Pilkington, C.M., Judaism. London: Hodder & Stoughton, 1995, p.98.

[26] Booker, Richard, The Miracle of the Scarlet Thread, Shippensburg, PA: Destiny Image Publishers, 1981, p.30

[27] Booker, Richard, The Miracle of the Scarlet Thread, Shippensburg, PA: Destiny Image Publishers, 1981, p.30.

[28] *Ibid.*

[29] CCC, Article 1343.

[30] Booker, Richard, The Miracle of the Scarlet Thread, Shippensburg, PA: Destiny Image Publishers, 1981, p.31

[31] Pilkington, C.M., Judaism. London: Hodder & Stoughton, 1995, p.98.

[32] CCC, Article 51.

[33] CCC, Article 292.

[34] CCC, Article 292.

[35] CCC, Article 374.

[36] CCC, Article 766.

[37] *Ibid.,* Article 1614.

[38] NAB footnotes commentary on Isaiah 14:12, 'Morning star: the king of Babylon. The Vulgate has "Lucifer," a name applied by the Church Fathers to Satan.' See New American Bible, p.893.

[39] The Douay-Rheims American Edition 1899.

[40] Majority of quotes courtesy of 'The Kolbe Center for the Study of Creation' with the exception of those drawn from 'Fundamentals of Catholic Dogma.'

[41] See also, OTT, Dr L., _Fundamentals of Catholic Dogma,_ Illinois: Tan books and publishers, Inc., 1960, p.79.

[42] OTT, Dr L., _Fundamentals of Catholic Dogma,_ Illinois: Tan books and publishers, Inc., 1960, p.95.

[43] _Ibid._

[44] Hahn, Dr Scott, _A Father Who Keeps His Promises._ Ann Arbor, Michigan: Servant Publications. 1998. P.81.

[45] _Ibid._

[46] _Ibid._, p.80.

[47] CCC, Article 701.

[48] Munk, Rabbi Michael, _The Wisdom in the Hebrew Alphabet,_ New York: Mesorah Publications, Second Edition, January 2010, p.148.

[49] Warkulwiz, Rev., V. P., MSS., _The Doctrines of Genesis 1-11,_ Lincoln, NE: Iuniverse. 2007. P.355

[50] _Ibid._, P.19.

[51] Hahn, Dr Scott, _A Father Who Keeps His Promises,_ Ann Arbor, Michigan: Servant Publications,1998, p.99.

[52] Cf. Warkulwiz,Rev., V. P., MSS., _The Doctrines of Genesis 1-11,_ Lincoln, NE. USA: Iuniverse, 2007, p.393.

[53] Warkulwiz,Rev., V. P., MSS., _The Doctrines of Genesis 1-11,_ Lincoln, NE. USA: Iuniverse, 2007, p.393.

[54] CCC, _Article 144._

[55] Booker, Richard, _The Miracle of the Scarlet Thread,_ Shippensburg, PA: Destiny Image Publishers, 1981, p.47.

[56] CCC, _Article 766._

[57] Booker, Richard, _The Miracle of the Scarlet Thread,_ Shippensburg, PA: Destiny Image Publishers,1981, p.48.

[58] CCC, _Article 270._

[59] Cf. 1 Cor. 15:34.

[60]Booker, Richard, _The Miracle of the Scarlet Thread,_ Shippensburg, PA: Destiny Image Publishers, 1981, p.48.

[61] Booker, R., _The Miracle of the Scarlet Thread,_ Shippensburg, PA: Destiny Image Publishers, 1981, p.53.

[62] Cf. _Psalm 76:3._

[63] Hahn, Dr Scott, _A Father Who Keeps His Promises,_ Ann Arbor, Michigan: Servant Publications, 1998, p.108.

[64] CCC, _Article 204._

[65] _Ibid.,_ Article 205.

[66] Carroll, Anne W., _Christ the King, the Lord of History,_ Illinois: Tan publishers, 1994, p.27.

[67] Buckingham, J., _A Way Through the Wilderness,_ Eastbourne: Kingsway Publications, 1983, p.47.

[68] _Ibid.,_ p.46.

[69] CCC, _Article 708._

[70] Pilkington, C.M., _Judaism,_ London: Hodder & Stoughton, 1995, p.184-201.

[71] CCC, _Article 700._

[72] Cf. CCC, _Articles 1472 and 1473._

[73] Pope John Paul II, _Novo Millennio Inneunte,_ para 30. I recommend reading paragraphs 30 through to 33 which treat of the universal call to holiness. This was one of the primary messages of the Second Vatican Council. It can be found in the document 'Lumen Gentium' and is restated in CCC article 2013.

[74] Greenberg, Rabbi Irving, _The Jewish Way,_ New York: Simon and Schuster, 1993, p.129.

[75] CCC, _Article 1375._

[76] CCC, <u>Article 633.</u>

[77] CCC, <u>Article 2017.</u>

[78] CCC, <u>Article 2018.</u>

[79] CCC, <u>Article 1987.</u>

[80] CCC, <u>Article 1988.</u>

[81] www.bridegroompress.com

[82] CCC, <u>Article 1994.</u>

www.ingramcontent.com/pod-product-compliance
Lightning Source LLC
Chambersburg PA
CBHW080754120726
48001CB00009B/2747